THE LIMITS OF REASON

THE LIMITS OF REASON

Indeterminacy in Law, Education, and Morality

John A. Eisenberg

Transaction Publishers
New Brunswick (U.S.A.) and London (U.K.)

Library of Congress Catalog Number: 91-24327
ISBN: 1-56000-017-1
Printed in the United States of America

Published in Canada by:
OISE Press
The Ontario Institute for Studies in Education
252 Bloor Street West
Toronto, Ontario
M5S 1V6

Library of Congress Cataloging in Publication Data

Eisenberg, John A.
     The limits of reason: indeterminacy in law, education, and morality/John Eisenberg
     p.   cm.
     Includes bibliographical references and index.
     ISBN 1-56000-017-1
     1. Sociological jurisprudence. 2. Law—Philosophy. 3. Moral education. I. Title.
K370.E36   1992   91-24327
340'.115—dc20   CIP

Contents

Acknowledgments

Though it is not possible to be aware of all the influences on one's thought, I am more than reasonably certain of my indebtedness to a number of colleagues. I am grateful to Jack Miller, Wayne Sproule, and Dwight Boyd for sharing their ideas on morality and education with me over the years. I am also grateful to Hesh Troper for insisting that moral theories and personal interest are not always separate in the academic world, in spite of what some scholars pretend. Clarence Joldersma was especially helpful in advising me on current theories of psychology, and in keeping in check some of the excesses in my treatment of cognitive science. I have also found Max Dublin's views on prediction to be useful and I benefitted greatly from Ian Winchester's and Heather Berkeley's suggestions on the manuscript.

Without his realizing it, Malcolm Levin has influenced my thinking as much as anyone from the time we worked on the Canadian Critical Issues series. Paula Bourne was also very helpful in her research of legal cases and in her suggestions on family law, even though I must take sole responsibility for the anarchic viewpoint infusing the presentation of the cases and their analysis.

I should also wish to thank Maier Deshell for his insightful comments and useful advice on the manuscript and Archie Rottenberg for the unconventional and imaginative ideas he has bombarded me with for much of my life. I am also indebted to Irving Louis Horowitz, president of Transaction Publishers for his valuable suggestions and warm support in the brief period that we have known one another.

Moreover, I wish to express my heartfelt appreciation to Beulah Worrell for the great effort she has given in preparing the manuscript. I also wish to thank Marg Brennan, Jill Given-King, and Stephen Hooker for their help.

Above all, I wish to thank my wife, Carol, to whom this work is dedicated.

Introduction

The Limits of Rationality

These are not the best of times. Neither space shots, genetic engineering, computers, nuclear reactors, general problem-solving models, television, electronic music, the Beatles, antibiotics, tranquilizers, supermarkets, capitalism, socialism, glasnost, the "triumph" of American democracy, nor encounter groups guarantee(s) good times. Nor do all together guarantee very much. If anything, the great scientific, social, and cultural breakthroughs of our age carry with them problems that seem to overshadow their benefits. But it is not the breakthroughs in themselves that create the problems. Rather, it is how we deal with these and other phenomena, how we view and assimilate them that is more decisive.

Because these are troubled times, law is important. So are the various "rational" ways we have of organizing society in order to keep the lid on. But law is especially so. This is not to say that law is important because it is needed to solve the problems we have or because it is the most effective way we have of controlling our collective destiny. In fact, I believe, the opposite is true. Because nearly everyone, certainly all politicians, *believe* that law is needed to solve societal problems, law is important today. As a result its role in society is greater and more pervasive than in better times. It affects in some ways everything we do, but not in the ways we think it does.

The common perception is that the purpose of the various forms of social order such as education, social decision making, and especially law is to improve things, to enable citizens to lead ordered lives and to avoid the chaos that the absence or insufficiency of these (and other) forms bring. This perception is reinforced in those instances in which laws do seem to make a difference, when palpable changes follow the introduction of new laws designed to bring about those changes; as when draft laws serve to get more soldiers into the army, or when seat belts laws seem to decrease traffic deaths and injuries, or in those rare instances where the introduction of capital punishment is followed by a decline in the murder rate.

But a better understanding of what law is and how law functions requires going beyond a few success stories. For it is not simply a question of whether the enactment of specific laws causes social outcomes that are considered good. It is also a question of what happens to our outlooks or consciousness and the very social reality we live in when many laws come into existence and when we deal with the world primarily in formal, legalistic ways. Perhaps most important for us today is what happens when law dominates social existence, when it is the basic way we have of conceiving and solving social problems—quite apart, as I noted, from what happens when law L somehow helps bring about change C. At its most general level my concern in this work is what happens when we are effectively dominated by a dogma of rational method in all social endeavours, not only law, when we view everything in fixed categories conforming to patterns of regularity that we can determine and upon which we plan our life activities. However, what we do not and cannot see is our own seeing and this makes life difficult for rationalists.

The view that all reality, including human and social reality, is at some ultimate level completely knowable, that all relationships and connections can be determined, that all social phenomena conform to general principles and laws, and that with knowledge of these humans can control their own destinies, is not peculiar to our own age. To some extent Plato and Aristotle shared these beliefs as did seventeenth- and eighteenth-century thinkers such as Bacon, Laplace, Spinoza, Gassendi, Leibniz, and many others. Perhaps the clearest and most uncompromising expression of this view is found in the writings of St. Thomas Aquinas. For St. Thomas, all reality is connected, everything is knowable, including facts and values, and ultimately everything can be set right. From God's Eternal Law everything follows, including Natural Law, or man's rational understanding of Eternal Law, and Civil Law. Not only can the nature of reality be logically derived from this, but so can the proper standards of behavior. All reality is a neat, determinable and rational system. Thus "man," who is a rational animal sharing in God's rationality can determine "his" actions in an effective and morally proper way.

As formidable and attractive as such a view may be in both scope and simplicity it is totally at odds with some of the most significant conceptions of our age that are based on what we know and have reason to believe we cannot know. The notion of a complete, self-sufficient, independent, objectively knowable order simply does not mesh with some of the most penetrating insights in mathematical logic, science, history, and anthropology (in its broadest sense). For example, Gödel, in his famous theorem, has shown that no complex formal or logical system is completable. In principle, some true propositions in every such system cannot be demonstrated, hence must be outside that system, unless the system itself is inconsistent. Thus no significant system is completely knowable, even by God, I might suggest. Hence a Thomistic world cannot exist. Heisenberg, in his uncertainty principle states that both the position and velocity of an electron are not determinable, in principle. Implicit in this view is the assumption that nature is *not* some independent entity open to discovery by the astute inquirer, but is dependent for its existence and character upon the technology or instruments used to study it. In effect, the very use of the instruments of measurement as well as the very observation of the inquiring scientists, cause changes in the system, hence partly constitute the natural system being studied. Thus, indeterminacy is built into scientific understanding in quantum physics. Similarly, McLuhan, in proclaiming that the medium is the message also claims that *how* we do things constitutes *what* we know. Thus the world of machine users is radically different from the electronic world of television and computer users. This is so because the environment, that is, those factors in the social context affecting human consciousness, are different in these worlds, hence the perceptions in mechanical and electronic societies are bound to be different. However McLuhan comes closest to an indeterminist position of sorts when he asserts that *prevailing* environments are invisible or unperceivable, hence we cannot be aware of the factors affecting our consciousness. As he noted, we do not know who discovered water, but we do know that it was not a fish. But once we do become aware of our environment, as we are aware of the way mechanical technology affects our perception, this environment no longer exists. If so, detached observation and reason cannot serve either as reflective mirrors or illuminating lamps of reality. For they are part of reality and make it indeterminate.

In the writings of such diverse thinkers as Spengler, Goffman, Illich, Beckett, Camus, Sartre, and others, elements of a world view or world views incompatible with the benevolent, objective, universal order of St. Thomas or Leibniz can be found. In these writings one can discern with varying degrees of clarity the personal and the external factors involved in our understanding of reality (whatever *it* may be) and in our dealing with it (if "it" is an it). The ungraspable, incompletable, inaccessible aspects of our being, the being of others and their interconnections are recognized and juxtaposed alongside the rational. As a result, a conception of reality that is neither ultimately knowable, controllable, nor good is emerging.

Yet the academics and politicians of our time overwhelmingly proclaim and practice rationalism. They analyze, categorize, correlate, formulate laws, then explain and predict and therewith attempt to control.

Simple, Clear, Powerful. However such a method is premised on there being completable, totally knowable, and externally manipulable reality. But, as noted, this view is at odds with other more plausible, reflective currents of contemporary thought. Quite simply, the prevailing academic approach is not compatible with some of the more fundamental strains of our knowledge and beliefs.

I suppose that I could recommend in rationalist fashion that academics and politicians modify their method. Or I could predict disaster and suggest ways of avoiding it. But this would involve my becoming what I am denying, and I still have problems with self-contradictions. This leaves me with the option of not creating a new system that begins by categorizing and ends with control. It restricts me to describing, telling, or narrating what I see happening and explaining this in various ways using intuition, reason, or speculation as the conditions suggest or perhaps, dictate. There still remains a significant rational dimension in my approach. This is probably unavoidable. However, such rationality, hopefully, will not be rigid dogma nor will it dominate to the exclusion of other ways of knowing. Nor will it be unaware of its own functioning.

To bring out the nature and consequences of the conflict between the dogma of thoroughgoing rationalism and the deeper structural and metaphysical conceptions implicit in the views of Gödel, Heisenberg, McLuhan, et al., I will try to make clear the assumptions, procedures, and limitations of the rationalist approach in the understanding and control of different areas of social existence. The areas I will examine and the problems I will deal with are those I have personally been involved with at various times in my research. By no means are these areas and problems exhaustive of social understanding. Our understanding of the economy, political forces, cultural phenomena, and many other aspects of society involve similar problems, as well as differences. However in dealing with rationalism in these areas I will try to depict the fundamental indeterminacy affecting all social phenomena, an indeterminacy that affects our very understanding of society and prevents any significant control of social outcomes.

In spite of differences among social realms as well as in the varieties of indeterminacy that infect them, one and the same phenomenon occurs, one basic principle holds. In all instances the means used to gain knowledge (or understanding), are themselves factors that prevent knowledge from being gained. Thus in a society where rationalism has taken hold of our thinking, where most decisions are made on the basis of rules, laws, principles, policies and so on, in order to control social outcomes, discrepancies between intended and actual outcomes consistently and necessarily happen, and will continue to do so.

The mechanization of the judgment process has taken hold in the dominant modes of contemporary psychology, in the teaching of morals/values in the schools, in institutionalized programs of penal and educational reform, in social and moral decision making and foremost in law. And the success rate in all these areas is, in my view, abysmal.

In cognitive psychology, human beings are defined as information processors, mind as brain, brain as computer. The role of mind in the creation of the theories they rely on is ignored as are the functioning of the theories they base their findings on and the rationality that permeates their consciousness. Likewise, in attempting to reform dysfunctional school systems and "deviant" students, educators ignore mind, theory, rationality, and even the functioning of the institution *in* which and *by* which (both!) reform is to take place. The promoters of moral and values education in the schools also use models of persons and methodologies in their programs, all the while assuming the autonomy and rationality of their students. Yet they too seem oblivious of the intrusion of the models, the rationality, the autonomous minds, and the institution of schooling on the process they are trying to manipulate with little or no success. But most seriously, politicians, jurists, legal scholars, and social reformers attempt to control individual and social behavior in society on the basis of the massive legalization of society, of subjecting social relationships and human interaction more and more to laws and legal procedures without considering the impact of the process they are engaged in and the means they use on society. Ironically, when faced with the vision of the failure of the system as when judges burn out, courts grind to a halt, or courts in Ontario are expected to drop as many as 150,000 charges (including assaults, rape, impaired driving, and possibly manslaughter charges) because the courts cannot deal with these cases within a reasonable time,[1] governments appoint more judges, create more courts, and devise more rules. Somehow, the thought of getting off the accelerating treadmill of law and legalization never occurs to our leaders.

Once infected with a measure of rationality, one cannot easily restrain it or limit it. It keeps growing. Thus prisons are built to control crime; crime continues to be uncontrolled and grows; then more prisons are built. Similarly fiscal policies to promote national wealth are put in place; in 1972 the national debt is seen as a serious impediment to national prosperity; more of the same policies of controlling interest rates, increasing unemployment, controlling inflation, and so on are put in place; and the national debt continues to grow, right to the present time. Admittedly, one cannot know how bad the crime rate or the national debt would be without the rational measures that have been taken in recent decades. However it is clear that rational planning has not yielded control. And the reason for this is that the means used, the mode of thought involved, the measures taken all affect social existence, yet cannot be taken into account in any sort of rational calculation. Yet any understanding of society and social forms requires an understanding of how the means employed affects the results of any action. This applies to any understanding of the human being, of mind and judgment, to the understanding of social reform, to the understanding of the educational process of how children learn and how they acquire values, and to how law operates in and affects our lives individually and communally. Obviously, these matters cannot be understood completely or even substantially. Perhaps such an understanding eludes us for the most part. In any event, no significant understanding of ourselves, education, or law can arise without some awareness of the indeterminacy endemic to social existence. But even knowing this will not carry us very far, certainly not to the point of being able to control our social existence.

Because I believe that there is a critical need to explore, as best we can the nature of social indeterminacy, how it operates what it affects and foremost why it exists, I will in the following pages undertake a preliminary probing of the phenomenon, or whatever "it" maybe. The areas I will venture into are not, as I noted earlier, unfamiliar to me, in as much as I have conducted theoretical research or carried out educational programs in the areas, or both. So I do have some direct experience in the sphere and with the indeterminacy that I believe operates therein.

First, I will refer briefly to the very curious area of cognitive science. This is an area in psychology that is supposedly at the cutting edge of science, with its use of computer models, not to mention its use of computer hardware, software and in-between-wares. It is a science that is supposedly contemporary in its outlook, yet it seems committed to determinacy, rationality, and probably completability. And though its mechanical achievements are impressive, its insights into humanity are nonexistent. Then I will consider the difficulties (perhaps the futility) of conceiving and implementing programs in moral education in the schools, aimed at bringing about individual or group development, an area in which I have had considerable first-hand experience. In effect, the problems facing moral education are the same problems of indeterminacy facing all education regardless of the area of study. I will next consider the nature and limits of rational decision making in dealing with social issues on both societal and personal levels. Formulae may be necessary for deriving valid responses in computers; they are useless in understanding conscious, functioning human beings. Finally, I will examine and discuss in some detail the nature of law as it functions in our society. As in the other areas, I will focus primarily on the major contradiction between what we believe we do and what we actually do in the realm of law. Then I will offer an explanation of why this occurs.

In all four areas common problems occur, suggesting similar deficiencies in approach. Very often, when specific rational procedures are followed to bring about specific desired outcomes, the outcomes differ from what is intended and what is expected. This discrepancy is not simply the result of an error in method or of some random happening as Burns suggests in his line "The best laid plans of mice and men gang aft agley." It may or may not have comforted the mouse to have known that among rational beings massive screw-ups are inevitable. If so, such discrepancies are tied to elements that are beyond the control of social reformers, educators, politicians, academics, and probably poets. In some ways the very structures used to bring about the desired results either obstruct the so-called "rational" achievement of the outcomes or create conditions that make the results unlikely. While each of the foregoing problems is distinct, all share one important feature, namely that the method or procedure used is inappropriate for achieving the desired outcome because of its own involvement in the process. Such a claim is not simply based on observations, but also on conceptual grounds. That is, there is some intrinsic logical incompatibility between what reason tries to do and what it can do. Rational method is premised on the possibility of conceiving and correlating all operative factors in a given process. But all such factors cannot possibly be taken into account. Reason cannot take reason into account any more than an eye can see itself seeing or a hand can grasp itself grasping. To some people this may seem rather arcane, like the obscure ramblings in an abstract Eastern philosophy. But it does have a practical payoff in that it accounts for the consistent and widespread failure of our most cherished approaches. While such matters may not help us make better decisions, they may serve to point out the dangers of systematic failures. Or they may not.

My claim that rational method militates against the achievement of the results it is designed to create is most readily shown in the field of law. As I earlier suggested, it is not enough to understand society solely in terms of specific laws achieving specific effects. What must also be considered is what the existence of law brings with it as well as how this existence affects specific outcomes. Likewise it can clearly be shown how institutional organization affects rational procedure. Thus it is one thing to have a rational plan for producing educated citizens, it is something quite different to carry this plan out in some social context. For the very existence of an educational system and a social structure within which it exists is bound to have an impact on or make a difference in the outcomes of that process. But how can one control the outcomes of one's environment if one *must* work *within* the context of that environment? Once again it is like the eye trying to see itself seeing. It cannot be done. Finally, I will maintain that rational decision making is limited in as much as it too cannot take into account the impact of its own existence in determining the outcomes to be achieved. To do so it would have to go outside of itself. Just as the instruments of measurement are part of Heisenberg's physical reality, so the rational mode is part of social reality. In effect, then, rational decision making has an added complexity, in that the decision made should take into account that a decision is being made, since the making of the decision is part of the relevant context. But the calculation taking into account that a decision is being made should itself be taken into account, ad infinitum.

For example, prior to a battle a general must not only decide how best to achieve a specific military objective, he (?) must subsequently take into account the effect his decision making as well as the decision making of others have on the ensuing course of events. To make the process even more complex, he must take into account what he believes to be his enemies' rational calculations, which themselves should take into account what his enemies believe to be his calculations. What makes such procedures so chancy are (1) they are incompletable because second, third, and fourth level guessing can go on indefinitely and (2) the very process of decision making must be taken into account, over and above the actual decisions made. But as I suggested, this is not possible, just as a hand grasping itself grasping is not possible.

In effect, rational decision making operates on several levels and cannot be seen as providing guaranteed solutions of specific problems. This complexity will be discussed in detail and illustrated with actual examples of social decision and policy making in chapter 3. I shall there contend that failure in rational decision making is often endemic or structural, and not simply due to procedural errors. In such cases it may be the result of a number of factors beyond human consciousness and control. On the other hand, successful rational solutions are in many cases (if not always) matters of coincidence. If so, the reason so many generals and corporate executives seem to lose their magical powers as time goes on is not because they are getting old, but because their luck has finally run out. Sooner or later the bullet will end up in the chamber in Russian roulette.

In summary, then, I will proceed as follows in this work. In chapter 1, continuing in the vein of this introduction, I will try to get as close to the primary source of indeterminacy as I can. Specifically, I will try to show that any attempt to see human beings or human minds as computers or machines and thereby base all social undertakings to control our future on the rational operations of mechanical or electronic machines is misconceived. For the human mind is not, nor can it be likened or identified with such machines or their programs. In chapter 2 I will discuss the effect of the structure of schools on moral education and penal reform specifically and on education in general. In doing so I will draw on Goffman's notion of the moral and institutional self, on Illich's concept of schooling and on my own experience in developing a program of moral education in a school for juvenile offenders to show that not only does the process of rational planning influence the functioning of any program, but equally the structure of the institution in which the program takes place determines the outcome of such programs. So once again more than rational conceptions go into the functioning of programs. In chapter 3, I will examine three fairly recent approaches to moral and/or values education that are widely used in North American and European schools. Each, in my opinion, fails to realize its goals because it either has an erroneous view of mind or fails to take its own rational mode into account, or both. Particular emphasis will be placed on a model of rational social decision making that I developed earlier on in my career. By applying this model (called The Strategic Reasoning Model) to political, technological, and social problems, I will indicate the limitations of not only this model, but also of this rational mode of solving such human problems. Chapter 4 will mark the beginning of the second section of this work and will deal primarily with law as a rational instrument of social change and control. In chapter 4, I will discuss Hart's rationalistic view that law is a system of rules. In chapter 5, I will discuss a second rational model of law, namely "law as determinate historical process." Then in chapter 6, I shall introduce the conception of "law in itself," or as one colleague termed it "noumenal law." Through this conception I shall attempt to demonstrate and account for the fundamental indeterminacy of law or even more poignantly suggest why law is so frequently a major source of anarchy in our society. Finally, in chapter 7, I will present a summary of the major findings of this work. In doing so, I will account for the indeterminacy in rational educational and rational social and moral practices and correlate this phenomenon with the indeterminacy of law. In effect, there are various factors contributing to the indeterminacy in education, social policymaking and law. But the result in all areas is the same. We cannot control the outcomes of our lives by rational means or methods. To believe that we can is the most dangerous delusion we can hold.

Frequently, the proponents of a rational natural order draw sustenance from Einstein's famous remark that God does not play dice with Nature. I disagree with this bit of Einsteinian wisdom. For I believe that Nature as we can know it, and human society even more so, is one big crapshoot.

Note

1. *The Globe and Mail*, Toronto, 27 March, 1991, A 10.

Part I

Reason and Control

Introduction to Part I

The great delusion of our times is that we can *in principle* bring about any change in society that we desire, if we know enough about ourselves and the conditions we live in as well as the laws and principles governing people and society. Thus educators commit themselves to the stimulation of the creativity of our children and to their moral, social, and cognitive developments. Likewise hucksters of every ilk and shade claim that by learning special kinds of thinking we can be in a position to solve all our problems and be on top of the world. And politicians and jurists believe that with a system of just, reasonable, and effective laws, law, order, and an attendant social tranquility will follow. But such self-assured promoters deceive themselves and everyone else.

This work challenges such naive beliefs and provides the theoretical basis for believing that such rational social control is not possible. Though some modest successes are registered in these areas from time to time, we are ultimately confronted by an intrinsic indeterminacy, an indeterminacy that precludes total, even substantial understanding and control of our destinies—even in principle.

1

The Cognitive Sciences:
How to Ensnare the Mind

Minds As Computers

I suspect that many scientists (and others) are spooked by that which they cannot control. To overcome this discomfort they must meet the perceived challenge to control what appears so elusive and difficult to control. But how can one even know, let alone control, that which itself is an essential part of the controlling? How can an eye see itself seeing? Cognitive scientists appear to have resolved this difficulty to their own satisfaction.

The most flagrant way of getting mind to grasp mind in its various modes is as follows. First define mind, ignoring all the warnings that this is a highly irregular, if not suspect procedure because it involves mind defining itself, without paying recognition to the fact that there is a mind defining. Second, determine the conditions that cause mind to exist. That is, find out what factors/conditions go into the making of mind (or minds). Finally, on the basis of the propositions you have established, in conjunction with relevant experiments, discover ways of producing those conditions that not only generate mind but that use mind to create desired outcomes or effects. In so doing, we know and control mind. That is, we come up with a clear conception of the entity (or process) mind and are in a position now to pull the strings governing its existence and operation.

This is, I believe, what cognitive scientists are attempting to do today. First they define mind variously as a computer, an information processor, or as the processes of a computer, constantly referring to some strange construct called "the computational theory of mind." What it comes down to, I would guess, is that they conceive of "mind" as either synonymous with "brain," or at least as essentially related to brain in an empirically determinable way. In doing so, they make the mind perceivable and possibly determinable. Then they conceive of the brain

15

as an information-processing machine. As a result, the mind is seen either as a machine in operation or as the patterns, procedures, software, or some other observable or scientifically determinable phenomenon. Finally, the actual workings of the brain-machine are studied—how information enters, is processed, stored, interpreted, produced, and ultimately used. The structures, procedures, and laws thereby determined are then related to the images or representations "in" the brain (or perhaps "in" the mind) and somehow connected to the outside world in which humans function.

Whether or not this is a parody of the computational theory of mind, some basic facts are indisputable. On this view, mind is reduced to chemicals or chemical processes and electrical circuits or their operations. Causation has been reclaimed from the moralists (e.g., R. G. Collingwood) and the legal theorists (e.g., H. L. A. Hart) who conceive causation in normative human terms. No longer is it necessary to mess our discourses on human beings and minds with such notions as free will, spontaneous decisions, choice, random behavior, and so forth. In principle, at least, control is just a switch away. To understand humans, study robots and computers. And to develop robots, study how humans function. After all, the two have been defined as synonymous or near synonymous. And what can be more authoritative than a fundamental definition?

That many cognitive scientists and their philosophical allies hold some such views is evident from the literature on the subject. For example Daniel Dennett writes, "What we want, in the end, is a materialistic theory of mind as the brain."[1] Another philosopher, John Searle seems to share Dennett's overall perspective when he writes, "Of course the brain is a digital computer. Since everything is a digital computer, brains are too."[2] And if the mind is something, it too would be a digital computer, on Searle's conception of the world. Similarly P. N. Johnson-Laird claims that

> what the computer offered—or rather the theory lying behind the computer—was a new conception of psychological explanation. This conception is much more powerful than the earlier mechanical analogies.[3]

So, to explain what the mind is, explain what a computer is. And to explain how the mind works, explain how a computer works. For the theory underlying each is identical. Such a claim is clearly compatible with an earlier assertion by Zenon Pylyshyn: "My proposal amounts to the claim that cognition is a kind of computation."[4] In his proposal,

Pylyshyn views human behavior—including what I am doing now and what he did when writing his book—as "a causal consequence of operations carried out on [specific] codes." Similar claims, variously qualified, have been made by John Anderson, John Haugeland, Jerry Fodor, Howard Gardner, and many others.

For the limited purposes of this chapter (ie., to show a fundamental weakness of cognitive science theory as currently stated) it may be fruitful to refer briefly to a recent work of Ray Jackendoff. In this work, Jackendoff explains all mental experience, all subjective awareness in terms of the computations of the mind. However, unlike those cognitive scientists who would reduce all experience to computations, Jackendoff believes that such phenomenological experience cannot be reduced to computations. Something more must enter in connecting computations to conscious experience. If so human beings may be something more than computers—though it is never clear what this is.

However Jackendoff is not prepared to give up the belief that there is an intricate causal connection between computations of the mind/brain and phenomenological experience.[5] This comes out clearly in his enunciation of the two fundamental assumptions (beliefs) underlying his position. First, he hypothesizes (believes?, knows?) that *every* phenomenological distinction is caused by, or supported by or, projected from a corresponding computational distinction. That is, each variation in our subjective experience or awareness results from a prior variation in the computations of the brain, which involve information structures and the processes engendering and sustaining these structures. In effect, human awareness is to some extent determined by the computer—mind/brain, and *every* change in awareness is causally connected with a computation arising out of a program.

In his second hypothesis (or assumption?) Jackendoff asserts that human awareness itself has no causal influence on behavior. Thus it is not one's awareness that a bear is walking in one's direction that in any way influences that person's change in direction and quickening-of-pace behavior. Rather it is new perceptual cues and the resulting information structure that cause him to turn around and climb the first tree that he sees. And so it is with all behavior. Awareness, consciousness, realization, and intention themselves do not change the world. New and processed information does.

The obvious benefits of such a view is that it allows us to correlate human behavior with clear and discrete programs, with codable information and processes sustaining that information. If social reality and human behavior can be seen in such clear, manipulable and manageable terms, then social reality and its attendant human activities can be depicted, explained, perhaps understood, and manipulated. In effect, it contains within it the promise of our ability to control our destinies. All we have to do is put the right program in place.

Unfortunately the problems with such theories are too numerous to recount in this brief excursion and too basic to enable the theory to be sustained with any credibility. Leaving aside such problems as making sense of a causal theory of behavior and the consigning of consciousness to causal limbo, when everyone knows deep in his/her heart that without consciousness there is no perception and without perception there is no information to be processed and fed into our mind/brain computers, I would only wish to point out a serious gap in the theory. While Jackendoff and his allies may study computations and the connection between these computations and human behavior, they do not get to the foundation of the very process they attempt to explain. What they fail to examine is the origin and generation of the very theories they base their positions on. One may reasonably ask where information theory has come from or what the origin of the computational theory of mind is. To raise such questions is to go to a level beyond the theory of cognitive science. For, even if one has all one's concepts, assumptions, rules of inference, and methodologies in place, one still does not know what the grounds of such beliefs are. For surely not every concept, rule, or assumption is acceptable. But to justify information theory or computational theory or cognitive science by information theory, is to argue in a crudely circular manner. Moreover to package that which gives rise to concepts as a concept is to distort "it." While using concepts to organize material *may* not be a fatal problem within a given discipline such as geology, paleontology, or chemistry, it is a fatal problem for any discipline that claims to investigate and systematize our understanding of mind. The most such a discipline can do is immobilize mind and treat it as an object observed. It cannot study mind, which in some metaphorical sense gives rise to cognitive science. For such a mind is prior to all categories and itself cannot be categorized. To do so would be to change it from active ground to passive object. Yet not to deal with this element — if only to say mind cannot be dealt with — is to omit the most critical aspect of mind. Incredibly, Jackendoff and his fellow cognitive scientists fail to deal with truly creative mind, active mind. If so, they do not provide us with a theory of mind or consciousness or awareness, but only with an outsider's glimpse of phenomena objectified and neutralized by the theories and structures they have contrived.

Compared to the theories of Jackendoff, Fodor, Anderson, Pylyshyn, and the others, the writings of Marvin Minsky are quite troublesome to philosophical indeterminists as myself. In my view, he is the most insightful and thoughtful of the cognitive scientists, and his basic position is unmistakable and uncompromising.

In one statement, Minsky states his position quite dramatically. Human beings are "nothing but computers made of meat."[6]

Thus, what minds are is no problem. "Minds are simply what brains do."[7]

Likewise, what brains are, is no problem.

> There is not the slightest reason to doubt that brains are anything other than machines with enormous numbers of parts that work in perfect accord with physical laws.[8]

Any attempt to view mind as somehow autonomous or transcending natural laws is unacceptable.

> I think that the idea that people have something like free will is obscene and disgusting. The idea that you have to make decisions for no reason just because it comes to you, to do this rather than that, that you're free is undignified. The fact is that you're just as controlled by the dirty little machines inside you as the dirty, evil untrustworthy people outside you. It's the nature of existence. The idea of free will is a laundering operation.[9]

To determine how the computing machine called the "brain" works or what laws govern the processes of the mind, one simply uses standard scientific method. The fact that mind is used to investigate mind makes no basic theoretical difference.

> Using the mind to examine itself is like science in another way. Just as physicists cannot see the atoms they talk about, psychologists can't watch the processes they try to examine. We only "know" such things through their effects.[10]

Thus psychologists proceed in the same way as all other scientists who cannot gain direct access to the phenomena they are investigating.

> How do you discover things about your mind? You make up little bits of theories about how you think, then test them with tiny experiments. The trouble is that thought-experiments don't often lead to the sorts of clear, crisp findings that scientists seek.[11]

Why are the results of psychological experiments so troublesome? Why do we become so easily confused, Minsky wonders? Why do we seem to trip on our own feet? In responding to these issues, Minsky seems, at times, to come perilously close to the indeterminacy I have been suggesting. But with his usual flair and self-assuredness, he avoids this pitfall.

Minsky clearly recognizes the distinctive problems faced by anyone attempting a systematic study of the mind/brain. Studying the brain, according to Minsky, is difficult because its processes are hard to classify. Studying brain processes is different than studying other processes.

> The difference is that brains use *processes that change themselves*—and this means we cannot separate such processes from the products they produce. *The principal activities of brains are making changes in themselves.* Because the whole idea of self-modifying processes is new to our experience, we cannot yet trust our common sense judgments about such matters.[12] [My emphasis.]

While I cannot accept the claim that self-modifying processes are new to our experience, inasmuch as the ancient Greeks and most societies after were aware of the paradox of the liar and other paradoxes wherein the utterance of a claim affected (even modified) its truth, I do find Minksy's dealing with the problem seriously somewhat impressive as well as unexpected.

In another section of the work, Minsky directly confronts the issue of the mind affecting that which it investigates. He notes:

> Our thoughts about our mind-experiments are mind-experiments themselves—and therefore interfere with one another.
>
> *Thinking affects our thoughts.* [My emphasis.]

However this, according to Minsky, in no way affects our ability to study mind and do mind experiments. To prevent such confusion, all a computer scientist needs is a special "interruption" machine which detects the intrusion of active mind on the mind experiment and thus enables the scientist to prevent or compensate for the intrusion. In effect, a serious philosophical problem is resolved by a technical device that no philosopher would recognize, let alone know how to use.

The upshot of all this is that Minsky can rest assured that cognitive science is safe from philosophical attacks. At worst, cognitive scientists merely have to learn to live with troublesome limitations. For there are limits on what consciousness can tell us about itself—because it can't do perfect self-experiments. This would require keeping perfect records of what happens inside one's memory machinery. But any such machinery must get confused by self-experiments that try to find out how it works—since such experiments must change the very records they are trying to inspect! We cannot handle interruptions perfectly. This does not mean that consciousness cannot be understood, in principle. It only means that to study it, we'll have to use the less direct methods of science, because we cannot simply "look and see."[13]

The brilliance of the foregoing explanation lies in its clarity in dealing with confusion. A positivistic methodology of science is posited, its rules laid out and problems of application directly dealt with. Thus if you cannot get direct access to your object of study, use the indirect method, that is, study *its* effects—as if there were an "it" in place producing effects and waiting to be detected. Furthermore, if your doing something necessarily intrudes on what it is that you are trying to do, get an interruption machine. (Is this anything more than a philosophical "fuzz-buster"?) That is, find a way of detecting the intruder and keep it out.

Unfortunately the matter is not that simple. First of all, the creation of an interruption machine is somehow due to a mind conceiving it. Not only is the experiment modified by thought affecting thought, but any attempt to deal with the problem, certainly one in which interruption machinery is conceived of and introduced, is affected by thought at a level *beyond the controllable experiment*. In effect, there is always one level beyond the level of operation of the cognitive scientist. Minksy's real confusion, I believe, is in taking a logical difficulty as an empirical one, as a difficulty occurring in a stable, preconceived context. The problem of mind grasping mind is not a problem of keeping the grasper from grasping. Rather, it is a *logical* problem, one that cannot be settled by some ingenious mechanical device. For mind grasping operates at a preconceptual level. "It" (if it is an "it") creates concepts and in this mode of operation, cannot itself be constrained or organized by a concept. To be detectable in an established system requires being classifiable. It is doubtful that the "mind grasping" is classifiable. Thus, whatever it is that Minsky's interruption machine detects, it is not (nor can it be) mind.

Finally, a somewhat distinctive conception of the mind that is partially at odds with the computational theory of mind has been put forward recently by the physicist and mathematician Roger Penrose. In *The Emperor's New Mind*,[14] Penrose takes a middle- of-the-road position on mind between the views of hardcore mechanists like Minsky or softcore mechanists like Searle and hardcore humanists, (perhaps like Sartre) who see the mind as arising spontaneously and independently. He rejects the mechanists for viewing the mind as a digital computer or information processor that proceeds from discrete state to discrete state. Such a view is clearly mistaken because the mind does not only operate as digital computers do in a linear logical fashion, deriving conclusions from premises and rules of inference. On the contrary, the mind can be shown to operate intuitively, to know certain truths without linear calculation. For example, Godel's theorem indicates that in every complex logical system, some propositions can be known to be true directly, and not on the basis of a linear calculation. If so, the mind does not simply compute in discrete logical stages. As well, Penrose rejects the humanist position for failing to provide cogent grounds for their mysterious conception of mind. However, his major focus is on finding a viable scientific conception of mind.

As a first step in coming up with such a theory, Penrose speculates that the mind can be understood as conforming, not to mechanical laws of nature, but to the fundamental laws of nature operating at the time of the Big Bang, at the time the universe originated. Penrose also holds that certain mathematical forms, which are as real as anything in external reality and the laws of quantum physics, are also relevant in understanding the mind.

Though the precise nature of the laws of the universe and the status of mathematics in reality are undoubtedly important for Penrose's theory, the concern in this section is more philosophical and less technical. In effect, my concern here is with the fundamental assumptions underlying his theory rather than with the technical details of the theory itself.

Fortunately, the nature of these assumptions was spelled out at a lecture he gave at the University of Toronto in October 1990 that I attended. During a period of informal questions, he made the following statement: "What I am doing in *The Emperor's New Mind* is developing a new model of mind."

To which I responded as follows: "What makes you think that the mind *can* be modelled? How is it possible to model that which creates models? Surely, the mind which devises or brings about or generates categories and models cannot itself be slotted into the categories it creates, and the models it generates? To do so, seems to me to be circular. It is wrong, because that which is modelled cannot be the mind I refer to."

In his response, Penrose stated that he understood what I was saying and that my argument had some plausibility, but as do all truly creative people, he said he would continue along the lines of the search he is now involved in. But as understandable as this reaction was, it did not deal with the basic flaw in his approach and of the approach of all cognitive scientists.

An Alternative to Cognitive Science Methodology

Criticism of the cognitive science view of mind and humans is not new. Nor has such criticism been effective—judging from the formidable influence of cognitive science on modern psychology as well as on social and military policy and programs. Cognitive science clearly delivers a product, whether it be an industrial robot, planes and tanks that "think," or models of how to solve problems. Something seems to be working—even though what is meant by "working" is not clear.

Somehow the arguments of dedicated humanists such as Carl Rogers, Jean-Paul Sartre, or Joseph Weizenbaum don't seem to influence anyone but the previously committed. To argue that humans cannot be compared to, let alone identified with, computing machines because humans have souls will not convince those who do not believe in souls. Nor does the argument that the way we understand and use technology (or anything else for that matter) rests on prior values that human beings spontaneously posit, sway those who view values as products of prior conditions. Similarly, the metaphysical-type argument that humans are unique in having personalties that enable them to define themselves and realize their aspirations seems unpersuasive to those behaviorists and cognitive scientists who believe that it is more beneficial to understand behavior as the result of conditions that can be analyzed and controlled than as the result of a disembodied, spectral personality.

Nor will my collection of reasoning, intuition, and polemic likely persuade any cognitive scientists, though it may help share my experiences and insights with those who are not at present antagonistic to my views. Perhaps the major difference in my argument is that I base it on work I have done in educational and correctional institutions, as well as on extensive research that I have done in history and law. I try to go beyond abstract metaphysical arguments about the nature of humans or moral arguments about the ultimacy of values. As a practitioner, especially in education, I tried to be sensitive to the methodology I used, though I couldn't keep out all basic beliefs, prejudices, and biases. In effect, the methodology I used was determined by what I had to do to understand and work with people in a variety of social settings. And this necessitated understanding *both* how people in social settings view themselves *and* how the mental world they live in could possibly exist. And both required active minds. Without such a concept, I could not deal with the situation.

Thus I was particularly drawn to a short section in *The Idea of History* by R. G. Collingwood. As a practicing philosopher, historian, archaeologist, amateur musician, and many other things, Collingwood was deeply concerned with methodological questions, primarily with the question, "How is one to study man and society?" In attempting to answer this question, Collingwood came across a number of the problems in the human study of human beings that I have raised in this work. And though I would disagree with a number of his assertions, I find his methodological focus to be a useful one, far more useful than moral or metaphysical arguments. But most important, I find his view of mind to be insightful and suggestive, even though one-sided and overstated.

For Collingwood, history is the study of mind, the reconstruction of the thoughts historical agents had in performing historical actions. According to Collingwood this is a relatively new area of inquiry and is as significant for twentieth-century thought as the scientific revolution was for the seventeenth century. In other words, a new element, indeed a new dimension of understanding has become the subject or our study, and this element is mind. The question thus becomes "How is mind to be studied?"

To answer this, Collingwood drew a contrast between science and history.[15] What does the scientist do in doing science as opposed to what the historian does in doing history? Collingwood's answer to this question comes down to a few specific principles.

Scientists proceed in three stages.

1. First, they establish categories into which all their perceptions can be fitted. Thus we have categories such as force, mass, acceleration, metals, electricity, conductors, and so on.

2. Then categories are correlated with one another. For example force, mass and acceleration are correlated in the formula "$f = ma$" or metals, electricity, and conductors in the statement "All metals conduct electricity." These statements or formulae are called laws.

3. Finally, using these correlations of categories, empirical phenomena are explained or predicted. Thus one explains why electricity flowed through some apparatus by noting that the apparatus was made of

metal and all metals conduct electricity. Or, one can predict that a circuit made of copper wiring will have an electrical flow because all metals (including copper) conduct electricity.

In contrast none of these procedures apply to history, because the subject matter of history does not lend itself to their application.

First, one cannot categorize mind in the same way as one categorizes inanimate objects such as metals, mass, or electricity. For mind is active and the basis of all knowledge. "It" *creates* categories; categories are not out there to be picked like apples from a tree. To categorize "it" would be dependent, hence to freeze "it," to make "it" passive. This would not capture the mind that knows, the mind that organizes experience.

Second, there cannot be laws of mind. If there were then it would not be mind that makes any choice, decision, or calculation. Rather, mind would be subject to other forces and mind would be dependent, hence irrelevant in any behavior. Thus to subject mind to laws is to render an active, dynamic element into something passive. It is also circular in that it is subject to the laws it somehow creates.

Thus, there can be no laws to explain or predict the operations of the mind. This is not to say that we do not anticipate people's reactions to events. For example, in a chess game each player will try to guess what an opponent will do; in wars generals make plans based on what their adversaries are expected to do; or in all human relationships one party tries to determine what the other will do or how he/she will react. But this is rational anticipation (which is open) and *not* prediction (which is closed).

In place of classifying, correlating, predicting, and explaining, historians try to reconstruct motives, perceptions, and calculations of historical agents using the informal "plain historical method," as Collingwood calls it. Through a study of documents and the use of human empathy, historians try to recreate Caesar's mind in deciding to cross the Rubicon. Only when one knows the genuine motives of an agent, can one know why an action occurred. Thus, Collingwood replaces the formal methods of natural science with informal empathy, intuition, and imagination in history.

When the methods of natural science are applied to human history, Collingwood believes the results are untenable. Likewise, he would believe that applying the empirical methods of cognitive science to the functioning of the human mind, to thinking, reasoning, planning, and so on is inappropriate. For one cannot deal with an active, dynamic process such as mind with frozen categories without distorting mind. Whatever it is that cognitive scientists and behaviorists talk about, it clearly is *not* mind. As Gödel has shown mind cannot be viewed simply as an object or process governed by rules and laws. Gödel's theorem itself is suggestive that a mind beyond the formal world of rationality is capable of grasping and/or generating fundamental truths, directly and intuitively, as Penrose has argued.

At its ultimate level, the human mind is that which gives rise to all the categories and constructs of the natural and social sciences. As such "it" cannot be dealt with in the same terms as the objects of inquiry in the natural and social sciences. Thus it cannot be dealt with by either physiologists, chemists, or cognitive scientists. And though the mind *can* be seen as not directly involved with the subject matter of physics, it *must* be seen as explicitly involved with the subject matter of psychology. If one probes sufficiently, one would come to the point of realizing that the mind at the core of inquiry is involved in the process of inquiry (or computing) being studied. The result is that a fundamental indeterminacy cannot be avoided, at some stage. For mind affects mind inquiring.

However, indeterminacy is not foreign to science, as modern physicists have shown. Cognitive scientists would do well to recognize this. They cannot put everything into a conceptual box. Try as they may to ignore it, they must sooner or later ask, "How did the box get there?" Their first impulse is to put the forces generating the conceptual box into a larger box. But where did the larger box come from? In time we will get a box within a box, within a box *ad infinitum*. But this does not answer the closely related question, "What came first, the mind or the box?" On this matter, cognitive scientists seem to believe the box came first, hence they never function without a box in tow (or a theoretical net, at least). However, I disagree with their approach. For some fundamental awareness or consciousness or mind *must* come first. For some such "thing" (or state or whatever) is logically and ontologically prior to the box holding the grasped mind.

Notes

1. D. Dennett, "Computer Models and the Mind: a view from the East Pole," *Psychology and Artificial Intelligence*, 14 Dec. 1984, 1453-54.
2. See D. R. Hofstadter and D. C. Dennett (eds.), *The Mind's I*, (Hammondsworth, England: Basic Books Inc., Penguin Books Ltd. 1981) 368, 372.

3. P. N. Johnson-Laird, *The Computer and the Computational Mind: An Introduction to Cognitive Science* (Cambridge, Mass: Harvard University Press, 1988), 23.

4. Z. Pylyshyn, *Computation and Cognition* (Cambridge, Mass: MIT Press, 1984) xiii.

5. For a statement of his basic theoretical assumptions, see R. Jackendoff, *Consciousness and the Computational Mind* (Cambridge, Mass: MIT Press, 1987) 276-77.

6. M. Minsky, *The Society of Mind* (Cambridge, Mass: MIT Press, 1989). Quoted in foreword by Martin Gardner to *The Emperor's New Mind* by Roger Penrose, xiii. Quoted in G. Murchie, *The Seven Mysteries of Life* (Boston: Houghton Mifflin, 1978). Reprinted in *The Globe Mail, Toronto*, 23 Jan. 1990, A 7.

7. *Ibid.*, 287, 288.

8. *Ibid.*, 288.

9. Quoted by Ian Brown, "Thinking Without a Brain," *The Globe and Mail*, Toronto, 6 Oct. 1984, 10.

10. M. Minsky, *The Society of Mind*, 60.

11. *Ibid.*, 58.

12. *Ibid.*, 288.

13. *Ibid.*, 58.

14. Oxford University Press, 1989.

15. See, R.G. Collingwood, *The Idea of History* (New York: Galaxy Books, Oxford University Press, 1989), 205-16.

2

The Moral Self v. The Institutional Self

Background

Although the inability of mind to grasp itself grasping is probably the most basic source of social indeterminacy, it is not the only source. For the factors that intrude upon human attempts to understand and control human existence are diverse. More than mind or human consciousness is involved in social action. For any social action presupposes a society with structures, rules, technologies for doing things, and languages to communicate with. That any or all of the ingredients that go to make up a society can be neutral instruments at the disposal of conscious rational beings for achieving their preconceived ends is not merely unlikely, it is impossible.

At the level of conceiving and perceiving the factors that constitute social reality, the mind is primary. It is the mind that creates categories and helps construct that reality. But in doing so the mind is incapable of constructing categories to ensnare itself in its activity for observation and examination. However indeterminacy does not stop there. Once social action begins—after all the basic conceptualizing, categorizing, and theorizing have been completed—a new type of indeterminacy appears. This is the indeterminacy connected with the organizational structures (or more simply, the institutions) erected to bring about change. For the institutions and other social forms that are created to implement our rationally conceived schemes constitute the very reality being modified, but in its operation cannot be grasped. Though institutions are quite different from minds, (and depend on minds for their existence) they function analogously to minds in being beyond the control of rational planning and action. Once again the means used to carry out rational plans are part of the reality the plans are aimed at, yet cannot be taken into account (as active means) in carrying out the plans.

If so, institutions can never be neutral or benign. They have lives of their own.

From early on, certainly from the time they start school, children in our society are trained to see and do things in a rational way. They are told that some sorts of behavior are good, others are bad. In time, the groupings of good and bad things grow until a plan or outline or model of acceptable behavior emerges. Almost exclusively the vision of children is directed outwards to existing values, given rules, and objectively discernible patterns of events. Rarely, if ever, are they asked to consider how *they* see and do things or whether their seeing and doing affects what they see and do. Rarely are these questions asked of anyone—adults or children. However in more recent times such questions have been asked on occasion by educators, philosophers, and social scientists. In asking such questions, they challenge the view that moral concepts and actions can be adequately understood by objective, rational observers and analysts. For nonrational elements enter the moral realm, elements that are nonobservable, nonobjective, and indeterminate. What these elements are and what their implications for education, particularly moral education are, will now be considered.

The ideas I wish to convey in this chapter have to some extent come about because of the experience I had working in a moral development *cum* social education program at St. John's Training School in Uxbridge, Ontario. Although my formal involvement at St. John's ended in 1978, my interest in understanding the total process, not simply the process defined by formal objectives and hypotheses, has persisted. And my belief now is that such a process is far more complex than outlined in the theories of moral and social education. The reason I believe this lies in the way institutions function in society, in the way they unobtrusively influence the behavior and social developments of those who use the institution to bring about outcomes that are rarely if ever realized.

Briefly, in 1973, Maureen Joy and I were invited by the senior administration of St. John's School to develop a program at the school along the lines of the Niantic program being carried out by Kohlberg, Hickey, Scharf, and their colleagues.[1] It was agreed that such a program would be carried out by regular St. John's school administrative, teaching, and line staff in conjunction with research staff and graduate students from the Ontario Institute for Studies in Education. The major objective of the program was to stimulate the moral development of the students from a predominately egocentric orientation to a conventional level of morality, and thereby reduce the likelihood of continuing antisocial criminal behavior. Because the members of the group were juvenile offenders between the ages of fourteen and seventeen, and were all involved in secondary school programs, we undertook to carry out a social studies program focusing on public issues in conjunction with the moral development program. It was believed that the skills developed in the public issues program would facilitate the judgments and decisions made in the moral development program and the experience in making practical decisions in the moral development program would help develop the skills needed in the public issues program.*

In many ways the program was a success. Groups of teachers, professional staff, and line staff were trained in moral development and public issues techniques. Cohesive groups of students, operating on cooperative principles of conduct emerged from fiercely competitive and hostile collections of individuals. A set of rules governing group conduct was conceived and developed by the groups. Violence in groups decreased to nil. Interpersonal problems were frequently resolved in a rational manner by the students. And in most cases, with notable exceptions, the students still remaining in the group at the end of the various programs revealed moral growth. However, because of the low numbers and frequent changes in group composition, no significant conclusions about the positive effect of the program on the students could be drawn.

And now for the bad news. In spite of recognized positive changes in individual and group conduct, some members of middle administration at the school remained hostile to the program. This group, comprised of section heads, their assistants, and school administrators was responsible for carrying out the daily program of the institution, and though it did not have the final say in matters of program and policy, some of its members were the real powers in the institution.

Though constant attempts were made to involve them all in conducting the moral development program, most remained distant from it. At first they stood back in silence observing the changes. After several weeks, when the program seemed to be working, they expressed doubts about giving power to juvenile delinquents, reaffirmed their belief in the old authoritarian approach, and even came up with their own theories of

---

*See chapter 3 for an account of the theoretical frameworks of the Moral Development and Public Issues programs.

rehabilitation, for example, "Run the asses off the kids so they'll be too tired to get into trouble" [actual quotation]. One official believed that discussion of issues and dilemmas only made the kids "mouthy." Kids like those at the institution needed more control, not more independence, regardless of what those professors say, he claimed.

In time, pressure on group counsellors to dissociate themselves from the program became quite intense. Often, programs were cancelled without notice and students were not freed to participate in group activities or for moral development tests. Not only did this disturb the students and professional staff, it affected some group counsellors most strongly since they were caught between institutional demands and their own commitments to a promising, enlightened new program. It was only a matter of time, in light of senior administration impotence, until the program was transformed by middle administration into one that was compatible with the old way of doing things and one that they could directly control. Though group meetings continued and some group decisions made, the just community or consensual democratic format gave way to a hierarchical system of control.

What I found most interesting, and often most perplexing, was the behavior of individuals under pressure in this context. Though students gradually developed a strong loyalty to the group and the moral development program and openly objected to unfair practices, they refrained from criticizing the institution and administrators, once they were led to believe that their release was imminent. A group head counsellor (the only university graduate among the counsellors) became agitated and upset when told by his superiors to disrupt the program. Intellectually, he affirmed his commitment to the program, but when he believed his job and social position in the community were in jeopardy, he went along with the superiors. At the other extreme, one OISE consultant reacted to the arbitrary administrative decisions by disobeying these instructions and in one instance threatened line staff physically if they continued to keep a highly agitated student in "the hole," that is, in solitary confinement. Of course this marked the end of the welcome of OISE student consultants at St. John's.

But even my own behavior perplexed me. From the outset I was committed to a determinate program and a determinate approach. During the crisis, I insisted that the academic program be continued at a reduced level, even though the students' minds were largely preoccupied with the administration-group conflict. I did not support the consultant who threatened staff and did not want to carry the struggle into the streets (i.e., go to the news media) as he insisted. I was constantly trying to get the planned programs on track after they had been derailed. But my doings, I can say in retrospect, were largely in vain.

Why the program went the way it did, why middle administration responded as it did, why students, consultants, professional staff, and teachers did what they did, is of acute concern for me today. It is obvious to me that these things cannot be adequately explained by existing theories. Certainly not by moral development theory. Behavior cannot be explained only by level of moral development. Other factors clearly enter. One has to do with the process of institutionalization, not only the nature of the institution involved. A second has to do with the complex of aspirations individuals have—that is, *their* good, not *the* right. And there are other factors.

In the following section, I would like to probe a bit more deeply into the institutional factor in the light of some relevant sociological theory. I would also like to examine the limitations of moral education programs which ignore the complex of aspirations and commitments people ordinarily have.

The Problem

In recent years educational theorists have shown considerable interest in the ways the structure of educational institutions affect education, especially moral education. For the most part, they have focused on the structure of the school and the way it determines what is learned by students. To guide their research, they asked a number of related questions pertaining to school structure and the learning of morality. Among these were:

•Does the school as institution affect moral education?

•If so, how does the structure of the school affect the moral content of what is learned?

•Is there anything in the structure or organization of the school that either enhances or negates genuine morality? —or perhaps the ultimate question:

•Given the way schools are organized and conducted, is moral education even possible in the context of schools?

To these questions, radically different answers have been given. Undoubtedly part of the disagreement is due to differences in the concepts used. Even so, genuine differences exist. At one extreme, Erving Goffman, using a broad conception of morality, believed that moral education *must* take place in the context of school activity, inasmuch as the school structure *constitutes* its morality. For there is no abstract genuine morality or moral principles apart from institutional structures. At the other extreme, Ivan Illich would *deny* that schools *could* educate morally. The very structure of the school precludes the learning of genuine humanistic values. Somewhere between these positions, Lawrence Kohlberg held that moral education is *possible* in the school, *only* if the school is organized according to principles of justice.

Underlying these and other positions are broader, more general assumptions. For example, underlying Kohlberg's views are philosophical conceptions of justice and psychological theories of how moral values are acquired. Similarly, Illich's views presuppose a humanistic conception of morality, a political conception of school and society, as well as a narrow causal theory of perception and learning. Both these approaches have received a great deal of attention in the past decade or so and are fairly well known. However, Goffman's position, though well known by sociologists, has not received the attention of moral educators, but has been virtually ignored. This is unfortunate, I believe, inasmuch as his underlying theory of the relationship between institutional structure, the self and morality is relevant for many of the issues discussed by moral educators and is suggestive of what can and cannot be done by such activities as school reform or institutional restructuring. More than any other theory that I have come across, it explains why sincere and well-motivated people cannot determine the outcomes of programs they initiate in total institutions.

Goffman's Theory of Institutions

In his seminal work *Asylums*, Goffman stated at the outset that "[a] chief concern [of this work] is to develop a sociological version of the structure of the self."[2] To achieve this end, Goffman studied the activities of inmates in various total institutions to determine how the structure of such institutions affects the very being of the inmates, including their moral natures.

According to Goffman, all total institutions develop the same mechanisms of control, the same patterns of relationships between staff and inmates, the same processes of induction into institutional life and the same sorts of operative values. Though Goffman's research dealt primarily with psychiatric hospitals, he claimed that similar phenomena occurred in *all* total institutions, whether they be prisons, monasteries, convents, army camps, boys' schools, or concentration camps.

Officially, every institution studied was set up to achieve specific goals, considered to be social goods. And officially, whatever went on in the institution was designed to realize those goals. In other words, the workings of the institution made sense and could be easily justified. Thus, Goffman, notes

> the various enforced activities [in the institution] are brought together into a single rational plan purportedly designed to fulfil the official aims of the institution.[3]

However in each and every institution conflicts arose between what the institution was supposed to do and what it actually did. Institutions that were set up to achieve certain goals were found, in actuality, to be pursuing altogether different goals. And where conflicts existed between official goals or policy and these other goals, the latter took precedence over the former. In effect, some unannounced, intrinsic pattern emerged and supplemented the rational pattern that supposedly prevailed.

According to Goffman, one basic fact, stands out in all total institutions. It is as follows:

> The handling of many human needs by the bureaucratic organization of whole blocks of people—whether or not this is a necessary or effective means of social organization in the circumstances—is the key fact of total institutions. From this follow certain important implications.
> When persons are moved in blocks, they can be supervised by personnel whose chief activity is not, guidance or periodic inspection but rather surveillance—a seeing to it that everyone does what he has been clearly told is required of him, under conditions where one person's infraction is likely to stand out in relief against the visible, constantly examined compliance of the others.[4]

In effect, a split results between staff, whose function is to control and inmates whose lot is to be controlled.

This in turn gives rise to the basic contradiction of total institutions, and to some extent, of all institutions.

> Many total institutions, most of the time, seem to function merely as storage dumps for inmates, but as previously suggested, they usually present themselves to the public as rational organizations designed consciously, through and through, as effective machines for producing a few officially avowed and officially approved ends. It was also suggested that one frequent official

> objective is the reformation of inmates in the direction of some ideal standard. This contradiction, between what the institution does and what its officials must say it does, forms the basic context of the staff's daily activity.[5]

In other words, in all institutional settings two conflicting moral orders seem to be functioning simultaneously. Overtly, the institution is designed to pursue a social ideal, such as therapy or reform or character development. But covertly, perhaps subconsciously, the institution serves to promote control. Where the two ideals or sets of values conflict, it is the pursuit of control that dominates.

Thus psychiatric hospitals that were initially set up to cure patients or restore their mental health often confine, restrain, or even mutilate patients by surgical procedures for the sake of "order," even though these actions are incompatible with improved mental health. Or schools, which are committed to developing the autonomy of students, systematically frustrate that development for the sake of order in the classroom and corridors.

Because such patterns are common to most, if not, all total institutions (and many nontotal institutions), it would seem that institutions have lives of their own, quite apart from the deliberate designs or structures imposed by their planners. In being organized into staff and inmates, in having to minister to the needs of blocks of people, and in requiring order to function, institutions carry with them a code that determines rules, roles, and relationships—in other words, a morality. Anyone participating in such organizations, necessarily partakes of that morality. The concept of individuals rising above the institutional structures and codes is an enticing one, but it is a romantic fiction. The very meaning of one's action depends on the meanings, hence rules, of the institution. Thus a person saying "Psychiatry is bunk" in a philosophy seminar may be seen as creative and insightful, whereas the same person saying it in a psychiatric setting would be considered recalcitrant.

Goffman thus concludes that there is no abstract morality apart from the structure of the institution, nor an abstract moral self independent of social institutions who share similar goals and values. This view is forcefully expressed at the end of a section entitled "The Moral Career of the Mental Patient" when Goffman writes that

> each moral career, and behind this, each self, occurs within the confines of an institutional system, whether a social establishment such as mental hospital or a complex of personal and professional relationships. The self, then, can be seen as something that resides in the arrangements prevailing in a social system for its members. The self in this sense is not a property of the person to whom

it is attributed, but dwells rather in the pattern of social control that is exerted in connection with the person by himself and those around him. This special kind of institutional arrangement does not so much support the self as constitute it.[6]

So if there is moral self, it is *constituted* by the arrangements governing moral activities. To live in society, is to function in a network of institutional contexts and to function in a network of institutional contexts is largely to be committed to the codes of those institutions. Of course conflicts are inevitable, because the codes of different institutions are contradictory, hence incompatible. But in the final analysis, it is the institutional structure, that is, the arrangements, the relationships, the rules and so on that constitute the morality. Morality thus becomes actual, concrete, not abstract and contextless.

It should be added, however, that Goffman's theory is not without its problems. For example, the methodology employed is often a hodge-podge of recollections, impressions, interpretations and literary anecdotes. Thus, the conclusions have not been "scientifically" (or adequately) established. Certainly alternative conclusions are possible. Even if a common pattern of relationships can be found in all total institutions, it is still possible that these relationships are the results of deliberate actions on the part of the members of the institutions who share similar goals and values. If so, it would be possible to avoid any undesirable consequences by taking into account these patterns and establishing rational procedures that make convivial and genuinely therapeutic institutions possible in some instances. In other words, it is possible to view the phenomena described by Goffman in terms of a rational decision-making model, a model in which staff determine institutional outcomes.

Perhaps. But my experience and the experiences of so many people frustrated by bureaucracies suggest something else. Given the pervasiveness of the control element in virtually all institutions,[7] one ignores at great risk the power of institutions or the institutional process. The human will is not omnipotent nor is the human being ever completely aware of the sources of his/her actions. Somehow, I am compelled to assume that phenomena outside my direct conscious perception occur—as Goffman claims. However, this is not to deny that the stated ideals and aims of institutions are totally irrelevant or inoperative, for boarding schools do differ intrinsically from prisons and convents from concentration camps.

Illich's Theory of School

One of the most penetrating analyses of how the structure of an institution affects its morality (or lack thereof) has been presented by Ivan Illich in *Deschooling Society* and several articles. However, Illich's concerns are not as general as Goffman's but are focused on the relationship between schooling, specifically, and values or moral education. Basically, he claims schools are undesirable because they *necessarily* carry with them morally destructive messages and values. Their very structure causes negative outcomes, which are unavoidable. He writes:

> In order to see clearly the alternatives we face, we must first distinguish education from schooling, which means separating the humanistic intent of the teacher from the impact of the invariant structure of the school.[8]

As did Goffman, Illich distinguishes between what individuals state to be their intentions and what actually goes on in schools. In short, he distinguishes between what one believes one is doing and what one is really doing in schools.

In fact, schooling itself carries with it, its own values program. According to Illich, the

> hidden structure [of the school] constitutes a course of instruction that stays forever beyond the control of the teacher or of his school board. It conveys indelibly the message that only through schooling can an individual prepare himself for adulthood in society, that what is not taught in schools is of little value, and that what is learned outside of school is not worth knowing. I call it the hidden curriculum of schooling, because it constitutes the unalterable framework of the system, within which all changes in the curriculum are made.[9]

The moral message foisted upon the students is neither benign nor open to the influences of the beliefs of the teachers, be they at the highest or lowest levels of moral development. For

> the hidden curriculum is always the same regardless of school or place. It doesn't matter whether the curriculum is designed to teach the principles of fascism, liberalism, Catholicism, or socialism; or whether the purpose of the school is to produce Soviet or United States Citizens, mechanics or doctors. What is important is that students learn that education is valuable when it is acquired in the school through a graded process of consumption; that the degree of success the individual will enjoy in society depends on the amount of learning he consumes; and that learning *about* the world is more valuable than learning *from* the world.[10]

Essentially, what schools teach is that power status is more important than quality of thought or value of beliefs, that knowledge is a commodity that can be quantified and packaged and that the worth of individuals can be determined by the quantity of the officially sanctioned knowledge they possess. No room is left for individuality, rebelliousness, creative reconceptualization, or imaginative activity. The values implicit in these views are incompatible with such genuine humanistic values as the dignity, autonomy and worth of all persons. Therefore the very structure of the school precludes the possibility of genuine moral education in schools.

Whether Illich's causal theory of the impact of structure on beliefs is correct or whether his humanism is acceptable is open to question. And without them, Illich's position would be clearly weakened. Somehow, Illich focuses narrowly and exclusively on how the structure of the school totally determines the content of what is learned. In doing so it blatantly ignores any connection between ideas and principles to behavior and the profound influence that personal commitments and beliefs have on human perception, learning, and action. Nonetheless, he does lend some support to Goffman's theory that institutional structures constitute accepted values, really an operative morality. Where Illich may differ from Goffman is in the belief that such a complex of values constitute a "genuine" morality.

Implications of the Analyses of Goffman and Illich

In conclusion, then, a number of implications will be drawn from the analyses of Goffman and Illich and the various observations and comments made:

•At the very least any moral system must be part of an institutional structure.

•This structure constitutes the group morality of those participating in it, whether they consciously choose it or not. It *determines* what really happens to individuals; rational, conscious individuals do not determine the most significant outcomes of their institutional lives.

•Though there may be individual or group deviations from official or dominant norms, participation in the activities of an institution entails at least some commitment to the existing structure.

•Individuals do not normally (or ever) partake of the activities of a single institution, but rather of a complex of overlapping institutions.

If so, the morality of virtually all people is comprised in part at least of the networks of rules and principles governing the operation of those institutions.

•Typically a young person may be a student, play sports in an organized league, have business dealings, work for a firm, belong to a union or employee's association, belong to a political party, associate actively in social groups and be a member of a reserve army unit.

Belonging to any or all of these groups entails being committed to a broad range of external rules, principles, conventions, and policies. The codes of behavior involved are not always, nor likely ever, consistent with one another. As a student in a moral development program, one is caught in a particularly nasty bind. On the one hand, one may be induced to *reason* morally at some postconventional or even conventional level, while on the other, one is compelled to *participate* in an authoritarian, materialistic, reward-based system.

As a member of a hockey team (or a wrestler, or a chess player) this individual is committed to winning. There may be limits to which any competitor may go in order to win, but the major objective is victory. Thus the offside rule is violated in hockey to give a team territorial advantage, personal insults are hurled at opponents to gain psychological advantage and injuries are feigned by players in order to create surprise. In effect, rules *can* never be seen merely as guides to specific ideals, but also as instruments to help them win the game. In the latter case the violation of a good rule is often seen as a good thing. "Good sports" and "bad sports" alike attempt to dominate their opponents, to defeat them, ultimately to render them impotent. In the extreme case of boxing, harming one's opponent is the goal of sport.[11] It is not the objective, nor a precondition of sports, to grant one's opponent maximum liberty compatible with a like liberty for all. When justice gets in the way of winning in sports, the goal to win almost invariably dominates.

In business, profit is the motive. The buying public is viewed as commodities. Subtle deception, called advertising and public relations, is practiced. Competitors are to be eliminated or restrained, if necessary and if possible. In the army, in times of war, opponents are often to be annihilated, rarely treated as ends making, autonomous beings, whose right to care or life is to be respected. In politics, the objective is to gain power. A former provincial cabinet minister, convicted of murder, went to the extreme of stating that

The battleground of politics is located in an area akin to the gutter of society. When it comes down to it, there are no rules in politics, and ethics are only for what may become public.[12]

Even one committed to democracy is *in practice* committed to defeating the attempts of opponents, to prevail politically. Even social situations are never nor can ever be free of the politics of domination. Friendships vary from mutually committed relationships to exploitive relationships—on platonic or sexual levels. Though one may feel guilty for failing to be completely altruistic in relating to others, it is doubtful that conviviality is achievable solely on the basis of altruism. No one I know would sincerely like to be a close friend of Mary Poppins.

•Unless human nature and society are radically transformed so that the objectives and rules of social practice are changed, there is no possibility of effecting a unity or consistency between moral theory and practice. The vast array of social practices that constitute social existence carry with them commitments to objectives, rules, conventions, and principles that are incompatible with the humanistic and developmental values that most moral theorists advocate. If society is to be transformed to such a moral level, sport as we know it will have to go, all competition would have to go, business would have to go, as would politics and probably sex. In other words, society as we know it would have to go.

•Tinkering with one institutional structure is likely to have little moral impact on society. Attempts to reorganize schools along consensual democratic lines or as so-called just communities may be futile for two basic reasons. First, such a structure is inconsistent with the structures and codes of most social institutions. Whatever may be learned in school—if indeed justice is learned—cannot likely be transferred to institutions where dominance, power, and materialistic values prevail. It would require abandoning almost all known social forms and practices. Schools, in the final analysis, constitute a small and insignificant portion of social existence for most people. And second, as Illich claims, attempts at school reform ignore the real power relationships and the underlying ethical and epistemological assumptions of the school. Given the roles of teachers and students in schools, it is evident that the student-teacher relationship cannot be the basis of a democratic institution. By its very nature, real power resides primarily with the teacher. In turn, the teacher is controlled in her relationship with administration, and so on up the ladder.

•Thus, it is with a good measure of scepticism, that I view the attempts of Kohlberg and his colleagues to produce morally advanced students through the reorganization of the school structure from its traditional authoritarian form to a just, democratic community where all individuals involved participate actively. Ostensibly, this position is buttressed by "research." Such research shows that "passage through [the] stages of moral development is facilitated by various processes." Among these is "[p]articipation in group and institutional structures perceived as fair or just." Such participation "stimulates moral development."[13]

Though I am not directly familiar with the Freudenthal and other research on which this is based, I would question the meaningfulness of findings that do not take into account the range of institutional structures operating in the subjects' lives and that claim that the structure of the school is perceived as just and fair. It is my suspicion that what the students or inmates had learned was verbalization of certain types of moral principles. I doubt that their fundamental social commitments were changed and ceased determining what they decided and did.

Such has been my experience in observing and working in the area. The tensions and contradictions I am referring to, emerge quite clearly in a videotape developed at the Niantic Correctional Institution for the demonstration of counselling techniques. Throughout the various segments on dilemma discussions, group problems, crisis intervention, and so on, a basic split emerged between the staff who held secure jobs in a state-run prison and inmates who would soon be forced to return to the insecurity of urban ghettos. In one dramatic segment, an inmate intimated that she would have to resort to prostitution when she left Niantic in order to survive. The head counsellor responded to this with righteous indignation, saying that she would think poorly of a person who did this. The narrator analyzed this conflict as being between higher (Stage 3, "nice girl") morality and lower (Stage 2, self-serving cooperation) morality. In contrast, I view it as an argument at cross-purposes, wherein the counsellor is arguing within the context of an abstract moral code and the inmate is arguing in the context of survival in a harsh urban society. No matter how elegantly one phrases the inmate's position it comes down to getting what she can by giving what she has. Otherwise she would perish. How could anyone outside that context pass judgment on her? Even so, it would not make any difference.

Similarly in my work at St. John's, I came to believe that changes in attitudes do not result simply from acquiring skills in an academic program nor by setting up a limited program outside the total social experience of its members. As noted in the introduction to this paper, students constantly had to deal with the conflict between the democratic structure of their dormitory group and the authoritarian structure of all institution-wide activities. Moreover, it seemed apparent that their experience in the moral development group at St. John's would have little or no effect on their behavior in the street society they would return to. Living in such a society carried with it many compelling commitments that differed from the abstract values that they learned to espouse.

Likewise staff in all its varieties had to contend with such contradictions. The OISE consultant, who was quite extreme in his resentment of all authority, especially repressive authority, could not really accept a democratic, discussion-persuasion mode of operation and in the incident referred to resorted to threats. Perhaps most complex was the dilemma of the head counsellor. As a member of a small town community he was committed to the codes of the various institutions he belonged to in the community— including the St. John's social community. As a person with a university education and with a moral code with a humanistic component, he was committed somewhat to the code of the program. The resulting conflict was, I believe painful to him, but ultimately his employment-social framework took precedence over a temporally limited academic intervention.

In my own case, I believe that my commitments to academia with the built-in elements of belief, ambition, and mode of operations came in conflict with the realities of daily experience. I was committed to an academic program of public issues discussion, to working with the ministry—*within* the system, had institutional aspirations linked to getting good results in my research, and so on. Though it never came to a showdown, I do not think that I would have permitted the program to be abandoned, even if the group as a whole decided on it. Even in moral development programs, in our society, some individuals have ultimate authority. And this is the source of the conflict between democracy as political theory and political reality.

In other words, our lives are comprised of many associations, many aspirations, many necessities, many codes of behavior. It is virtually impossible that a time-restricted, abstract, general-code will influence the palpable realities of other experiences. If so, I am forced to draw the following conclusions from all this.

Moral education programs in the schools are either futile or severely limited because:

(a) The *structure* of the school, especially the implicit power relationships, is a morality in itself, quite apart from the *stated* morality of the school, and almost always takes precedence over the stated morality; and

(b) The *content* of the morality in moral education programs is in conflict with the more powerful content of the dominant operative moralities of the major institutions of our society. Thus there is a pervasive indeterminacy in social practices, in the sense that we cannot determine our own ends deliberately and rationally. For we are constrained by the life we live. In some instances we are born or thrown into life-long settings not of our own choosing. At times, we are drawn to a life-style irresistibly. Occasionally, we consciously decide to join a social group. But in all instances there is a significant similarity, namely, structures impose values without our consent or awareness. We have no choice but to conform because we can only reject societies, not Society. No imposed, rational educational program can much affect this state of affairs.

Notes

1. L. Kohlberg, P. Scharf and J. Hickey, "The Justice Structure of the Prison: A Theory and an Intervention," *The Prison Journal* 51, 2 (1972): 3-14.
2. E. Goffman, *Asylums: Essays on the Social Situations of Mental Patients and Other Inmates* (Harmondsworth, England: Penguin Books 1961) 11.
3. *Ibid.*, 17.
4. *Ibid.*, 18.
5. *Ibid.*, 73.
6. *Ibid.*, 154.
7. In my personal experience the element of control was apparent even in such institutions as Niantic, The School Within a School in Brookline, Mass. and the Cluster School in Cambridge, Mass., where so-called just communities or democratic groups were established.
8. I. Illich, "The Alternative to Schooling," *Saturday Review*, 19 June, 1971, 45.
9. *Ibid.*, 45.
10. *Ibid.*, 45.
11. See Brenda Jo Bredemeier and David L. Shields, "Values and Violence in Sports Today," *Psychology Today*, October 1985, 123-32, for a discussion of the values and reasoning of athletes. The authors note that "intimidation, domination, fairness and retribution are continuously woven into [sport] participants' fabric of thought." (29).
12. Colin Thatcher, *Backrooms, A Story of Politics*, (Saskatoon, The Western Producers' Pairie Books, 1985). Quoted in *The Globe and Mail*, Toronto, Nov. 4, 1985, A5.
13. L. Kolhberg, P. Scharf, and J. Hickey, "The Justice Structure of the Prison, 2, 3.

3

Moral Education Today:
Control Through Reason

The Hidden Agenda of Formal Education

In spite of all the rhetoric that school administrators, professors of education, and classroom teachers utter about human freedom, student participation, self-esteem, self-actualization, independent learning, and critical skills, the ultimate goal of education yesterday, today, and tomorrow is control. The concern is not simply with keeping order in the corridors, schoolyards, and classrooms. It has to do in some way and to some extent with the ultimate in control, the control of the mind.

To get control of the mind, it is widely believed that one must have detailed theories of the mind and models of the mind. With theories and models, one is able to know how the mind works, what it does and why it does it. Only then can one know which conditions are needed to bring about desired outcomes—right across the curriculum. Thus with the right theories, models, and conditions one can stimulate cognition of all sorts, artistic abilities, social relationships, and even proper moral behavior. For every endeavor that the mind is involved in, there is a system of control. But the ultimate in such control is moral control, that is, getting students to do what is said to be right.

In my experience at least, the major thrust in formal education since the 1960s, if not earlier, has been to control morality by making it rational. It may not always work or ever work, but it is the central aim of formal education. Of course no principal or teacher or anyone in the system will admit to it. As I noted, the rhetoric is about autonomy, skills, and feeling good about yourself. However no school system I have seen would tolerate a permissive, open morality that *can* go with genuine student autonomy and self-actualization. What schools require is a conformity to a social morality that is generally acceptable, one that promotes the existing social and political order, respects certain traditions, values, reason, and civility and eschews drugs, violence, and other antisocial acts. Schools do not tolerate disruptive, fiercely independent behavior regardless of its intrinsic merit.

Control, however, is not a particular behavior that can be described by an observer in a situation. Rather, it is a relationship that results from a complex set of activities and relationships in a system. Thus control in education is the power that authorities or administrators or teachers have in bringing about some preconceived state or conditions. Control is manifested in those situations where specific outcomes result from specific programs. In such instances students develop cognitively because of a math or science program, groups develop socially because they are given the responsibility of designing and justifying their own class programs in social studies or they develop morally to higher stages because they discuss dilemmas and participate in a just community or consensual democratic group process. Effectively, control arises in the context of a system. In education, the dominant belief is that control arises in the context of a rational system that includes a specific scientific method whereby patterns of observable behaviours are established, hypotheses are tested, rules of logic are followed and so on. When the foregoing method, with its assumptions and norms, are used, the desired outcomes are expected to follow. According to B.F. Skinner, the phenomenal progress in science in the past four hundred years is due to the use of this method.

In spite of Skinner's claim, it is far from obvious that this method is even valid or acceptable. It has been contended in the previous chapters that the method is basically flawed and that the claim that we can produce desired social outcomes using this method is false because such a method does not and cannot take its own operation into account in its own operation. Quite simply a fundamental indeterminacy precludes the possibility of predicting and controlling outcomes by the use of some rational method of inquiry. Whether or not this is the case with moral education in the schools today is the subject of the following discussion. Have recent programs in moral education succeeded, as their advocates claim? Can such programs seeking the control of morality, of mind in some sense, achieve what they set out to achieve?

Historical Background

The following sections of this chapter will have a slight autobiographical element in them in as much as they relate to moral/values education programs I either used or developed or both. To some extent the comments reflect my own subjective response to the programs. But they will be more than subjective. There will, in addition, be an academic aspect to the discussion, in which I analyze and present a critique of the various programs in some detail. Though this section ties in closely with the theme of social indeterminacy, its major focus will be educational, hence will primarily be of interest to educators and those members of the public concerned with educational issues. And though the central hypothesis of this work is supported in this section, one can scan it or even omit it without missing the major thrust of the work.

The moral/values education programs that I shall discuss first entered the public education scene in the 1960s. In spite of the aura of radicalism and novelty surrounding these programs, each contained a significant rationalist component, each was concerned with bringing about moral and social improvements, hence each was committed to the control of educational outcomes—as were most of the programs of the time. The 1960s and much of the 1970s were times of the New Curriculum with its attempts to rationalize mathematics in the New Maths, science in the New Science, the social studies in the New Social Studies, and in effect, all inquiry. A common U.S. reaction in the late fifties and early sixties to the early Soviet space successes was to panic into the belief that the Soviet educational system was superior to the American system. The response of leading educators, including Jerome Bruner, was to launch a so-called new form of rational education that emphasized critical thinking, the empirical method and the learning and application of general laws and principles. Thus, the so-called "New Curriculum."

Perhaps the major intellectual source of the vaguely defined theories of the 1960s was the pragmatism of John Dewey. Dewey did not have much patience for the niceties and subtleties of metaphysics. Instead he advocated an educational system based on direct human experience, reflection on this experience, and practical achievement. Learning, knowledge, or understanding did not involve abstract speculation but rather doing and succeeding in actual life situations. Thus the major activity in education was problem-solving. For Dewey, to solve a problem properly (or rationally, as I would put it) involves going through five steps, as follows:

> 1) *suggestions*, in which the mind leaps forward to a possible solution; 2) an intellectualization of the difficulty or perplexity that has been *felt* (directly experienced) into a *problem* to be solved, a question for which the answer must be sought; 3) the use of one suggestion after another as a leading idea, or

hypothesis, to initiate and guide observation and other operations in collection of factual material; 4) the mental elaboration of the idea or supposition as an idea or supposition (*reasoning*, in the sense in which reasoning is a part, not the whole of inference); and 5) testing the hypotheses by overt or imaginative action.[1]

To educators, Dewey's lockstep system for solving problems has enormous appeal. It provides a sequence of steps that is general enough to apply to all situations and in doing so enables one to control nature as well as the student trying to control nature. By operating at both levels, the procedure solves the problems of problem-solving, as well. In such a procedure, patterns of regularity (general hypotheses) are sought, regulated reasoning is carried out, nature and society are controlled for human ends, and in so doing problems are solved. To me, this appears to incorporate the essence of rationality. Not surprisingly such a view has influenced Bruner's structuralism, Fenton's Mode of Inquiry and Herbert Simon's General Problem Solving Model[2]—all of which have had considerable impact on North American educational theory and practice.

Given the firm and extensive commitment to experience-based rational problem solving, it is not surprising that such models were applied to many different areas of the curriculum. I suppose that the ultimate in rational problem solving would be to apply the models to all areas. So what began as the New Mathematics was extended to the New Physics and shortly thereafter to the New Social Studies. Some educators even extended this approach to the arts. However the most striking extension of the view that intelligence, knowledge, or understanding *is* (or is essentially related to) problem solving occurred in the area of moral or values education.

It was to a backdrop of the broad and diverse concepts of the New Curriculum that the most recent attempts to develop programs in values or moral education arose. Though most (if not all) of the programs claimed a debt to Dewey's theories, the differences among them were as striking as the similarities. They differed on the place of affects or feelings in morality; they differed on the meaning of rationality, problem solving, and the self; they differed on the place of reason in morality, and on much more. Thus the basis for preferring one approach to values education over another was quite complex. In retrospect, my choice of a program was determined largely by a notion of rationality as problem solving—a notion in keeping with the times. To the extent that other approaches were at odds with the notion, they were either qualified or rejected.

In the late sixties, three approaches to moral/values education dominated the field. Though each approach had its strengths, I found two of these largely unacceptable and as a result devoted my research time and energy to help develop the third approach. However in the course of developing such a program, problems intrinsic to rationalism emerged. To indicate, what such problems may be, let me now present and discuss in some detail the three approaches—Values Clarification, Moral Development and Public Issues. In my view, each approach was a reasonable response to existing problems in education. Yet each response gave rise to new problems, which were be at least as serious as the problems it responded to. Each was oblivious to the limitations of reason.

Values Clarification

On the surface, Values Clarification (V.C.) appears to be a benign, nonintrusive, liberating, and uncomplicated approach to values education. It says all the right things about the validity of students' perspective, the importance of experience in learning, and the nonintrusive role of the teacher. Thus it appears to be as open and nonmanipulative as possible. However, only after one examines it closely and sees it in operation can one know that it does not and cannot realize its conflicting goals of problem solving and student-centred, autonomous clarification of values. For it has neither a valid model of rational problem solving, nor a means of reflecting on the operation of its own procedures. Thus it satisfies neither rationalists nor indeterminists.

However V.C. is perhaps the most popular and widely used program of values education in the United States and Canada. Initiated around 1965 by Louis Raths, at Columbia University, V.C. was set up as an alternative to the traditional didactic, teacher-directed, unreflective and abstract approach to the learning of values in the schools. By drawing on Dewey's notion that "the raw materials of life experiences" should form the basis for learning values, the humanistic notion of the self-actualizing, autonomous person and the democratic political notions of the rights of all members of society, Raths developed an alternative to the old-fashioned sermonizing programs (as in the earlier McGuffy readers) that prevailed up to that time.

In the Introduction to *Values and Teaching* (lst ed.) the authors state that they are presenting "a theory of values and a methodology for the clarification of values." But it is not an abstract theory of values nor a mechanical method of clarification that they are discussing. Rather they are primarily concerned with the practical activity of people understanding and using values in the context of their living experiences. As a result there is a theoretical and practical dimension to their work.

Underlying V.C. is a network of related concepts. At the core of the theory is the concept of the human being or the person. Using a contemporary humanistic conception, Raths et al. affirm the ultimate value of the human being who is autonomous, hence capable of making free choices and giving meaning to one's life and the world. Human autonomy is never to be compromised, for to do so is to demean the human being. As humans, we need—in fact have a right to—validation and respect. This entails showing respect for the autonomy of others.

On such a theory, choice becomes a central factor in human experience. For in a world where we are constantly confronted by problems at a personal, social, or even political level, we must learn to make choices in order to act. This is not a simple matter because the world is complex and confusing, and confusion leads to error, apathy and often destruction. To avoid such consequences, we must learn to clarify our values. Otherwise our actions are rudderless, undirected. They go nowhere. Hence by coping with confusion, V.C. is an important instrument or device in human existence.

But what are values? Raths and colleagues recognize that there is no consensus as to the meaning of the term. "Values" means different things to different people, thus they do not attempt to impose a firm definition on educators. However in general terms, they see values as "guides [which] tend to give direction to life [and] growing from a person's experience." Thus "values are part of living."[3] As such, an important part of values is to take action in order to solve problems. To be effective in guiding our lives values must be clear. In this regard, the indebtedness of V.C. to the pragmatism and values theory of Dewey is apparent, on a general level at least, if not in all particulars.

Raths et al. also provide seven criteria for determining values, which together constitute the progress of valuing. Briefly, they are "choosing freely. Choosing, from among alternatives. Choosing after thoughtful consideration of the consequences.... Prizing and cherishing. Affirming. Acting upon choices. [and] Repeating."[4] In effect, valuing entails choosing, thinking, caring, being committed and acting on the values repeatedly. For example, one truly possesses charity as a value only if one repeatedly chooses to perform charitable acts and does not merely say one believes in charity. In effect there are cognitive dimensions to valuing as when we reflect and choose; there are also affective dimensions to valuing as when we feel deeply and care about our values; and there are social, pragmatic dimensions to valuing, as when we act upon our values. Underlying this view of human choice, affirmation, and values is the belief that under the "right" conditions, each person can be in control of his or her activities, of his or her destiny. But what are the right conditions?

On this theory one can achieve a state of liberation and control through a process of values education. Essentially this form of education is the process of clarifying one's values. Students become engaged in this process by clarifying their beliefs, prizing values, choosing values, and finally by acting. Vehicles for engaging in these procedures are the exercises in works like *Values Clarification*[5] by S. Simon, L. Howe, and H. Kirschenbaum. In these exercises students are asked to consider whether they think teenagers should choose their own clothes, children should be raised more strictly than they were, or religion is important. They are asked to rank order the importance of the space program, poverty program, and defense program and their preference for a cat, a dog, a turtle, and a parakeet. They are also asked to list twenty things they like to do, to list three things they like about another person and to decide who among a group they would give preference to for a heart transplant. And other mentally demanding exercises—exercises where they can never be wrong.

In all instances of valuing, the autonomy of the student is paramount and never to be compromised. The role of the teacher in values education is to help students make choices through teaching the process and facilitating clarification. However, the teacher supposedly never imposes his or her values nor controls the process the student is engaged in. Thus Raths et al. reject those forms of values education that point to examples set by adults or that point to good models of the past or present such as Washington's honesty or Mother Theresa's saintliness;[6] that persuade or convince others by presenting arguments and reasons for this or thaot set of values...,"[7] that appeal to conscience, impose rules or that in any way constitute methods of control. Teachers are never seen as manipulators in this program. They never judge, only accept. All they do is help the student get to know what she or he is about.

Thus there is a strong relativistic element in V.C. On this view the individual is the ultimate judge of what is right for her or him. Values are not matters that are true or false. They are products of our experiences hence are "personal in nature." For everyone must "prize for himself [and] choose for himself."[8]

As a pragmatic, experience-based program, V.C. is ultimately to be judged by its outcomes. For

> the major hypotheses of values clarification [is]: If a person skilfully and consistently uses the "valuing process" this increases the likelihood that the confusion and conflict etc will turn into decisions and living that are both personally satisfying and socially constructive.[9]

In fact, the supporters of V.C. report positive results from the use of the program. They have found that students in the program tend to have clearer goals, are happier, are more energetic, and deal more effectively with their problems.

From the foregoing, it should be apparent why V.C. appeals to some educators (though not all) in the humanistic tradition. It is an approach that focuses on the perspective and judgment of the student, hence is student-centred. It is an approach that seeks harmony and avoids conflict. It is accessible to teachers and no extensive training program is required. And finally, it is compatible with "the democratic ideal" in which the rights to be respected and to make free decisions are central.

However not all educators, nor even all humanists find this program to be an adequate form of values education. Though criticisms have come from different quarters, from rationalists and nonrationalists, I shall confine myself to a few concerns of each.

To the ethical philosopher, one problem is that V.C. does not distinguish the moral from the nonmoral, that is, decisions arising out of conflict situations based on principles and decisions about preferences where no conflict is involved and no principle of conduct is involved. Furthermore, the trivial and the important are treated on the same plane as when students decide between a cat and a parakeet as a pet, or the space and poverty programs. Too often, the major concern is with trivialities and rarely with serious social problems.

More seriously, V.C. treats all positions and all procedures as equally valid. It seems to claim that you cannot be wrong, if you are clear. Students are asked to clarify, not to justify—except as a means of clarification. As a result the force of reasoning is never considered, the criteria of selection or choice never examined and evaluated. It is no wonder, then, that Raths et al. lump programs that indoctrinate together with programs using persuasive reasoning as unacceptable alternatives to V.C. But surely, any self-respecting rationalist would claim, persuasion based on sound reasons and evidence is not to be associated with dogmatic, unreflective programs that force doctrines on defenseless students. The former is legitimate and part of the long tradition of western intellectual thought. The latter is not, because it reduces the human being to an unthinking, unreflective object.

The rational deficiencies of V.C. is further underscored in a film entitled *Using Values Clarification,* where Sidney Simon presented a rank-ordering exercise to a group of students. In the exercise, students were asked to determine which of the following is "the stupidest"—a thirty-year-old man who started smoking after stopping for a year, a teenager who resents having to wear a safety helmet and refuses to do up the chin strap, and a woman suspecting breast cancer who refuses to see a doctor because she is terrified of being seen nude. One student said the woman is the most stupid because doctors have seen many nude women. Dr. Simon praised the student for letting us into her thinking process and asked rhetorically "Who among us can tell her she is wrong?" In making this statement Dr. Simon was reinforcing the V.C. principles that the student's reasoning is beyond question and the rational persuasion is unacceptable. Unfortunately, Dr. Simon's rhetorical question does warrant an answer. Any rationalist could say "I can tell her she is wrong. Her reasoning is weak. Jack the Ripper may have seen nude women, but that does not make him the right person to see for a medical diagnosis—even if he were a medical doctor." What V.C. entirely overlooks, indeed neglects, is the rational force of people's choices and judgments.

In this same film, Tom Erney, a school counsellor in Florida concludes the discussion by claiming that V.C. is the only program that teaches decision making. This claim is, I believe, false. To clarify values is not yet to reason or even think properly. To achieve "thoughtful consideration" one must not only clarify one's belief, one must understand the validity of the principles underlying one's argument as well as the force of one's arguments. V.C. may achieve the first of these. It fails to address the other two. It lacks rational force.

Finally, there is the problem associated with the attempt to control moral or value outcomes by means of rational structures and

---

Using Values Clarification (1975), produced by Dave Bell Associates, Hollywood, Ca., Distributed by FILMS INC, Chicago, Ill. Distributed in Canada by Visual Education Centre, Toronto.

principles. As noted, despite its rejection of all forms of control, rational and nonrational, V.C. seems to recognize rational control at two levels. First, students control the outcomes of their choices by using V.C. techniques and exercises. Second, V.C. programs are involved in the control of student behavior by being the cause of positive outcomes in their lives. It is this second type of control that constitutes a serious problem for V.C. In effect, a theory, techniques, materials, classrooms, and so on form a system that, it is argued, produces greater happiness, effectiveness, clearheadedness, and energy. Surely such a structure constitutes a controlling force in the cognitive and affective lives of students, in contrast to the stated principles of the program? If so, then V.C. is an intrusion on the process of autonomous value clarification. In effect, the V.C. program serves as a means of *directing* valuing, hence choice. Contrary to this, it has been argued throughout this work, that the level of spontaneous activity of the mind cannot be intruded upon rationally. It is that which conceives spontaneously. It cannot be that which is controlled. If so, the claims of V.C. effectiveness are meaningless.

Moral Development Theory in Education

At about the same time that moral educators in North American were first exposed to the soft, permissive humanism of V.C. a much more rigorous and systematic approach to moral education was also emerging, namely the Moral Development (M.D.) theory of Lawrence Kohlberg. Whereas V.C. is more widely used by teachers, the moral development approach is more widely accepted by academics and theorists. Of all the theories of moral education, M.D. theory is most extensively worked out, most widely tested by empirical studies, most widely discussed by educators and as a result most criticized and defended. To understand moral education in our generation, one must understand M.D. theory.

The major reason that Moral Development theory appealed to so many educators and academics is that it attempted to reconcile the phenomenon of human rationality with scientific method and a natural order. To put it crudely, M.D. theory (as does Cognitive Science) made thinking scientific; or tried to do so, without mangling or distorting the inner force of thinking. It began by defining morality as moral reasoning, "discovered" the patterns in which reasoning developed, then determined the conditions that affected the process of moral growth both positively and negatively. In effect, it tried to use its knowledge of how moral reasoning develops to control moral reasoning. As with V.C., reason was used to control morality. And as with V.C., the theory asserted that it was based on a belief in the autonomy of the moral person. A serious issue arising in M.D. theory was, thus, whether the system of rational control was compatible with the assumption of the autonomous moral agent.

To carry out so grand a project, Kohlberg drew on Dewey's notions of experiential learning and problem solving and Piaget's theory of human development. Kohlberg tested his theory of how children progress morally in a longitudinal study, confined to male subjects (to his everlasting regret). He also carried out validating research in many different societies, including the U.S.A., Taiwan, Mexico, Israel, and Turkey. Thus he claimed to discover a basic pattern of development of all human beings regardless of place, time or particular cultural conditions. In effect he sought to reveal the inner structure of rationality and its externally perceived order of unfolding. In so doing, it not only claimed to reveal what morality objectively is, it also claimed to reveal what ought to be, based on the natural order.

Underlying M.D. theory are various fundamental conceptions.[10] Kohlberg maintained that there is an invariant pattern of human growth based on the natural order of things. That is, humans develop in the same general pattern, both cognitively and morally. Humans, thus, have an innate capacity to grow morally, if conditions are right, and should not be viewed as being permanently locked into rigid categories or stages. According to this developmentalist view, all people evolve in their moral reasoning in distinct phases, from lower to higher states. Because this process of development is shared by all people, these phases are seen as natural and not as artificially contrived. Each phase is called a "stage." Empirical evidence in support of such development has been found, it is claimed.

The second concept in M.D. theory is "moral." According to Kohlberg, the moral realm is the realm of interpersonal value conflict. To resolve such conflict rational principles of "rightness and fairness" are needed. On this view, conflict is at the heart of morality. Thus, when individuals or groups are in conflict, when their objectives and values are at odds, the need arises to resolve the conflict rationally according to general principles. Ultimately, the principle that should determine how the conflict is to be resolved rationally and properly is the principle of justice. Morality, then, is part of the human realm and has to do with what is right, what we ought to do. This, according to Kohlberg, requires the use of rational principles and good reasons.

Each stage in our rational development is an organized system of thought. It constitutes a way of seeing the world. In effect, a stage is a way of organizing the multitude of thoughts and perceptions in our consciousness, so that we can make sense of what happens in the world and subsequently act in the world. It is conceived by some as a *gestalt* or pattern or structure. It is not a substance or thing.

In the moral realm, a stage is characterized by the *type* of principle used to resolve conflicts. It has to do with the *form* of reasoning imposed by such principles. As such, Kohlberg's theory is a formal or structural theory. Thus the traditional virtues such as honesty, industry, obedience, and so on do not form the essence of morality. The kinds of reasons used do. For being honest, in itself is not a sign of high morality. If one is honest because one fears punishment (or wishes to hurt others) one is not as moral as one would be if one were honest out of respect for others. If so, the *kind* of reason or principle or structure of thought determines morality.

There are, according to Kohlberg, six stages of moral development. The first two stages constitute a preconventional level of morality. At this level, individuals are only interested in how they are physically affected by their actions. Egotistical concerns are primary, not social concerns. Stage 1 is called "the punishment-and-obedience orientation" and reflects a deference to physical power, be it a parent, king, mighty warrior, or Rocky. Stage 2 is called the "instrumental-relativist orientation" and reflects a greater awareness of how others can be used to achieve mutual benefits. However, at this stage there is no commitment to others. One's only concern is one's own physical well-being. The next two stages constitute a conventional level of morality. At this level, one goes beyond one's narrow physical interests and recognizes the needs and interests of others in one's family, social group, or nation. Loyalty to others emerges. Stage 3 is called the "interpersonal-concordance orientation" and one's behavior is guided by how it pleases others in the group and how it helps one's group. At this level one's primary concern is to be seen as a "good girl" or "nice boy." Stage 4 is called the "law-and-order orientation" and it reflects an emergence beyond exclusive loyalty to one's friends and family. It also reflects a commitment to the needs of the state and a recognition of one's duties to others in one's own society. In most societies, few individuals develop beyond this stage. The last two stages constitute a postconventional level of morality the highest level. At this level, one goes beyond the needs or interests of fixed social groups and makes decisions on the basis of universal principles of morality. Stage 5 is called the "social contract, legalistic orientation" and at this stage one recognizes the existence of a universal social contract based on the greatest happiness for the greatest number principle. Stage 6 is called the "universal, ethical principle orientation" and moral reasoning on this level proceeds on the basis of universal ethical principles that apply equally to all human beings, are compatible with fairness or justice and require (in a moral sense) that all humans be treated as ends-making beings, never as objects. Higher stages are logically possible, though sufficient empirical evidence does not seem to exist for such a stage, nor even for Stage 5.

The sequence of development of all people is invariable, hence one progresses through the stages in a definite order, beginning at Stage 1. It is not possible to jump over a stage. The reason for this is that each stage is an attempt to resolve the inadequacies of the previous stage. Thus Stage 3 directly resolves the problems of Stage 2. Stage 4 does not; it only resolves the problems (or contradictions) implicit in Stage 3. In effect, we grow when a given structure breaks down and is seen as inadequate and a new structure that resolves the inadequacies is found. So development takes place in a logical order, in the context of personal and social conflict.

Each person can reason at the dominant stage of his or her development, as well as all stages below. As well, each person can comprehend the reasoning one stage above his or her own. Thus growth can occur. However, it is futile to preach to students at the highest moral level when they are at a Stage 2 or 3 level. Most people, when confronted with the moral statements of a Buber, Gandhi, Martin Luther King, or Dietrich Bonnhoffer translate or reduce such statements to the terms of the stage they operate in. They are not yet ready to understand the reasoning underlying the actions of moral giants.

In contrast to the relativism of V.C. theory, M.D. theory denies the view that all moral positions are equally valid, that values are personal matters, and that each person has the right to determine what is right. Such relativism (really subjectivism) is erroneous because it fails to recognize the process of moral development that all persons go through and the greater adequacy of the principles used at the higher stages. Rather, M.D. theory maintains that there are universal criteria of morality that can be shown to be more adequate than others. Moral rightness is not simply a matter of personal taste or preference—as when one prefers blue over green or chewing gum over potato chips.

One's stage of moral development can be determined by a standard moral development test. Such a test is comprised of a series of moral dilemmas and questions pertaining to the dilemmas. The responses are classified according to standard procedures and the test has emerged as valid on the basis of standard statistical criteria.

One of the major controversies surrounding M.D. theory pertains to the place of action in morality. It has been argued with some force that *what one does* forms an essential part of morality, not *how one reasons* as M.D. theory claims. To this criticism, two responses have been given. The first is that *why* one does something determines *what* one does. That is, the motive forms the essential part of an action. Thus if X gives Y $100, it is necessary to know whether X was paying back a loan, X was bribing Y or Y was robbing X, in order to understand the natural of the action. Similarly in moral matters, why one is acting determines what one is doing. Motives cannot be dismissed as being separate from action, nor from morality but constitute the essence of each. The second response is that there is a positive correlation between the stage of moral action and charitable, altruistic acts. Individuals who reason at higher stages of morality tend to behave more morally towards others.

It should be noted that moral development does not occur spontaneously, without causes, nor totally randomly. A summary of research carried out by psychologists and educators in a variety of contexts suggests that at least four conditions are necessary in most instances for moral growth.[11] Very briefly these are:

•One must discuss personal and social dilemmas, have one's views scrutinized and respond to criticisms.

•One must be exposed to higher stage principles than one's own. Otherwise one's existing views would be reinforced or go unchallenged.

•One must experience active role taking. That is, one must have social power and responsibility, hence make decisions and be held accountable in order to develop morally.

•One must function in a social context that one perceives to be basically fair and just. Individuals cannot develop in a context that is seen to be totally corrupt.

If the goal of education is to promote moral, cognitive, social, and even aesthetic growth, knowledge of these conditions is critical for educators. It is important to note that the conditions promoting moral development are not Skinnerian stimuli nor mechanical causes but involve human perceptions, interpretations, conscious relationships, and reasoning. They involve rational, sensitive persons. Thus, according to Kohlberg, if schools are to be effective means of stimulating moral growth they must be organized *not* along authoritarian lines, which are antithetical to such conditions, but rather as a just community that functions along consensual democratic lines and requires the active involvement and caring of all students and staff.

In conclusion, then, it would appear that Kohlberg has devised a formidable rationalist theory of morality and education, a theory that contains the elements required for the rational control of the process of moral growth. It is a theory anchored in reason and in empirical fact. It carries with it the assurance that schools can promote moral growth among children, if only the structure of the school was just and the program right. But as noted, it has been criticized from many perspectives. In this section, I wish only to mention a few of the criticisms I have of this system reflecting both the rationalism and antirationalism that coexist uncomfortably in my thought.

First, an opinion I hold as the result of observing M.D. programs in the context of just communities. Over the years I have conducted a M.D. program at St. John's school, Uxbridge, Ontario. I have observed meetings and classes in the prison setting at Niantic, Connecticut, in the "just community" in Cambridge, Massachusetts in the School within a School Brookline, Massachusetts, and at St. John's School, Uxbridge, Ontario. In all instances, I have found the experiments to be unsuccessful in spite of what their promoters claim. As I noted in the previous chapter, purely academic, rationally conceived programs are doomed to failure because they do not, indeed *cannot*, take into account the intrusion of the institution and of conflicting moral values that are incompatible with our stated values. To some extent, my perceptions of all these institutions (and others) confirm my claim. In this criticism, the irrationalist in me is speaking.

Finally the rationalist in me has its own difficulties with M.D. theory. In spite of Kohlberg's claims that M.D. theory focuses on moral reasoning, he fails to do so. In describing the stages or in analyzing arguments, the most that Kohlberg does is describe *kinds* of reasons or types of principles. He does not provide the criteria of *actual* moral reasoning. For example in the debate over capital punishment, one can argue for capital punishment on the grounds that it will promote law and order and one can argue against capital punishment on the grounds that it will undermine law and order (by providing a bad example of legalized killing). By not providing some means for deciding which argument is better, M.D. effectively fails as a viable mode of problem solving. Clearly more than a label for the *type* of reason used is needed to resolve moral conflicts. Because M.D. fails to provide the criteria of moral reasoning, or the mechanism of moral reasoning, or even indicate what it would look like, it fails as an adequate rational approach to moral education, if indeed rational approaches can be "adequate."

Furthermore the two arguments connecting moral reasoning to action fail. The first response founders because it merely shows that all conscious actions are necessarily infused with motives, but having a motive or reasoning in a certain way is not yet to act. If so, Kohlberg's theory is not connected to practice, only to theory. Moreover, positive correlations between stages of reasoning and action is not yet a necessary connection between the two. Thus Kohlberg's theory suffers because of its weak connection to actual human behavior. It is essentially abstract theory.

Finally the indeterminist in me rebels against Kohlberg's manner of dealing with reasoning. By observing the reasoning of subjects, classifying such reasoning in terms of a priori or fixed categories, and correlating these categories with other categories such as conditions stimulating or inhibiting development and finally explaining or predicting behavior on the basis of the correlations, Kohlberg merely deals with thought as static observed entity, not as spontaneous, dynamic object. As I stressed repeatedly in previous chapters (especially in chapter 1) there is a difference between a hand grasping and a hand grasped, between an eye seeing and an eye seen. Even more significantly there is a difference between "reasoning observed and packaged" and "the ungraspable dynamic reasoning" taking place, the reasoning which actively probes and solves, the reasoning at the core of morality. Kohlberg merely discusses the former, not the latter. Yet it is the dynamic reasoning that constitutes moral decision making. It alone is the essence of morality, if there can be such an essence. It cannot be packaged neatly or categorized. It is simply *not* that sort of thing. So, whatever it is that Kohlberg is discussing, it is *not* morality.

Canadian Public Issues

A third approach to moral/values education to emerge at the time was the Public Issues Approach. It was initiated in the early 1960's by Donald Oliver at Harvard University[12] and developed into a number of diverse programs and theories in the U.S.A., Great Britain, Canada and elsewhere. On this approach, values education was based on the discussion of actual controversial issues arising in the society in which the student lived. In such a program students learned how to take a position on matters of social conflict and to support and defend these positions.

The specific theory and program I will focus on in this section is the Canadian Public Issues (CPI)[13] program, an offshoot of the Harvard project, developed at the Ontario Institute for Studies in Education in Toronto, from 1968 to 1980. In my view, it is the most acceptable *rational* form of values education, though it suffers from the sort of limitations that all rational approaches do. Though not as blatantly as M.D., it attempts to control morality by making morality rational—something morality is not and cannot be. CPI also fails to take the impact of the institution and of the rational method used on the outcomes of its program. However, it is the most open of all moral and values education in taking seriously the autonomy of students. Unlike V.C. and M.D. programs, it makes no clear or explicit claims about trying to bring about behavioral changes by such programs. It is based on the commonsense pragmatic view that one learns to deal with personal and social problems by actually dealing with them in a consistent, critical way. Whether or not this is so, will be discussed in some detail in this section. However what is of special interest to this work, is that the CPI program reveals the working of special form of indeterminacy when two or more "autonomous, rational" individuals are engaged in a conflict, in competition with one another. If this is so, then the method of rational analysis and discussion, is not a reliable way of forming policies and programs aimed at bringing about desired goals. For such outcomes are indeterminate.

Unlike most moral/values education programs, The Canadian Public Issues Approach is *not* meant to be a self-contained and comprehensive course of study. But in many respects it is similar to other programs. It focuses on valuing as does Values Clarification. It stresses reasoning as does Moral Development. It uses conflict as a source of ethical discourse as does Moral Development. And it uses discussion as the primary mode of interaction as do Values Clarification, Moral Development, and most other programs of values education.

Moreover, CPI along with M.D., V.C. and most other programs associated with the New Curriculum were reacting against an outmoded form of education—something more suited to nineteenth-century rural society than to the twentieth-century industrial, "scientific" world. They criticized education in the 1950s and 1960s

- for being didactic and treating students as passive receptacles to be filled with factual information;
- for being authoritarian by setting the teacher up as the infallible authority and discouraging questioning of data, critical judgment, and independent inquiry;
- for focusing on memorization of "fact" as the primary method of learning; and
- for being abstract and not related directly to the daily activities in the lives of students.

In place of this antiquated education, they advocated

- student-centred education that was relevant for their life interests;
- action-related education that was experiential and had planned outcomes and benefits;
- Independent-reasoning that focused on structure, critical thinking, and problem solving; and
- the fostering of creativity in the natural sciences, social sciences, the arts, and the humanities.

Thus there is a loosely shared humanism, pragmatism, and rationalism among the various approaches and programs.

But CPI is also distinctive in a number of significant ways. Its distinctiveness lies in the way it uses existing disciplines, in its development of cognitive, decision-making models, in its conception of the process of practical reasoning and in the range of materials it has produced.

Thus CPI should be viewed neither as identical with any other program, not even the Harvard Public Issue Program, nor as a packaged program that fits into preordained slots in the curriculum. Rather it is essentially an approach to education as well as a means of achieving specific educational objectives. It does not exclude the use of other approaches, though it limits their use. However at a most basic level, its philosophical assumptions are distinctive and differ radically from those of any other existing approach.

As an approach based on contemporary humanism, CPI holds the view that human beings are distinct from objects and other beings in that they are capable of spontaneous thought, of making free choices, setting goals, and choosing values. According to this view, all moral choice is based on human freedom. As humans we have minds, we are aware and are capable of thought; we can make judgments and decide on courses of action. Only because we have such freedom, can we be responsible for what we do.

To be an object governed by laws or conforming to given patterns is not to be free. Such objects, whether planets orbiting the sun or animals (or people) controlled chemically, cannot rightly be held responsible for their actions. In contrast human beings are thrust into this world, as Sartre says, "condemned to be free." Paradoxically, on this view "we are not free not to be free"—at least as agents.

This is what it means to be human. For all human beings, the humanity of others, must be dealt with in a special way, or else we violate their humanity. We don't treat humans as we treat objects. We take their spontaneity into account, and take their "being" into consideration.

As a result, all humans are seen to have obligations to others by virtue of their being human. This means not treating others as objects but as subjects capable of setting values, making choices, and acting. This in turn means recognizing the rights of all to realize their freedom, "their right to care and concern," and their right to dignity. It ultimately means recognizing the rights of all human beings, to hear others, and be heard with respect. The denial of this right and its corresponding obligation is a violation of the humanity of others (though sadly it may be an expression of the humanity of the denier).

In human society, the most characteristic (if not essential) activity is *dialogue*. Through dialogue we interact consciously with others. We listen and are listened to respectfully. In dialogue the meaning we give to the world is communicated to others, who may share in that meaning. Dialogue is a special human relation. Genuine dialogue is not simply an exchange of words or sentences. It involves understanding what others are saying, of sympathizing with their feelings and their views—even when disagreeing with them. Otherwise how could one respond meaningfully to another? In effect, dialogue is communion, a uniting in thought. It is not the submission to the thought of others.

There can of course be disagreement in dialogue. Freedom virtually guarantees diversity of views and thought. But disagreement is not the same as disrespect. On the contrary, in genuine dialogue people disagree and try to persuade (though not manipulate) one another because they believe one view is right. Likewise, in dialogue people can be persuaded without being compromised and ultimately the various individuals can reason together, develop together, agree or disagree and act, despite Raths' misgivings about persuasion in *Values and Teaching*.

Too often debate is confused with dialogue, making points with gaining wisdom and understanding, manipulating others with being right. Such confusions are perhaps the greatest dangers to authentic education. However if such confusions can be avoided and surmounted, genuine dialogue can take place and genuine education result.

Finally, two important implications for education of the humanism of CPI should be noted. First, values education programs such as V.C. that claim to be nonjudgmental and accept *all* views as equally valid are mistaken. In accepting all views, they *are* being judgmental. Moreover in accepting all views they would accept Nazism and all other forms of oppression that deny basic humanistic values. Thus they are caught in a self-contradictory bind on two counts. Second, any program that employs a precast, deterministic, scientific framework (be it a rigid behavioristic or a more subtle developmental framework as M.D.) is also unacceptable. Such programs treat morality and decision making as observable objects of study subject to natural laws (or as conforming to patterns of behavior). Such approaches fail to take into account the spontaneity and freedom of moral agents, which are unobservable. Because of this, scientific approaches fail. From the foregoing it is evident that CPI comes closest to the recognition of the fundamental role of the mind in conceiving and perceiving the work and in making choices and acting in the world. It tries to avoid control by adopting a rational method of dialogue. However it does not recognize the indeterminacy involved in using this method.

On a practical level, a number of key concepts form the working framework of the Canadian Public Issues program. In brief, these are:

Definition

In general terms, as noted, the CPI approach is one in which the various positions and perspectives in controversial social (or public) issues are discussed, analyzed, justified, and, if possible, resolved. The treatment of such issues is seen as a major component of all forms of social education.

Programmatic Flexibility

Though CPI is often conceived as part of Canadian Social Studies, its methodology and approach can be extended to other subject areas (e.g., English Literature, Law, History, Physical Education, Science, etc.) In all these subject areas the same sort of rational resolution of problems is central.

However it should not be treated as an independent moral or values education program. It is widely recognized today that all education is moral education. Thus it would be educationally unsound to claim to deal with values only in one program when values form part of all programs. Values can be adequately dealt with in the existing curricular structure, though in some contexts courses in ethics could be of supplementary benefit to students with special philosophical interests.

Normative Focus

CPI is, however, not a traditional social studies, law, history program. Traditionally social studies were descriptivist in nature and were considered to be neutral in orientation. This approach was implicit in Mark Krug's claim[14] that historians in their inquiries ask three main questions:
- "What happened?" (i.e., the facts).
- "How did it happen?" (the mechanics).
- "Why did it happen?" (the explanation).

However CPI asks a fourth question:
- "Was it right?" or "Should it have happened?"

This last question adds an important normative, perhaps *moral* dimension to social studies. It involves dealing with values in whatever context they arise. It involves making judgments on the appropriateness and rightness of actions taken in society—in the past, present and even in the future. In so doing students are not limited to studying the facts.

Thus when an industrial program affects the environment, a political or military struggle occurs, a decision to prolong the life of a suffering person is made, or the rights of a person are denied in the name of public safety, value judgments can and should be made. However, in so doing one should go beyond the values of the parties involved in such conflicts. Ultimately one should invoke principles that one accepts as right or just.

Goals of the CPI Program

Basically, a CPI program has two goals or general objectives. The first is tied to content (i.e., factual knowledge is to be learned). The second is tied to process (i.e., cognitive and social skills are to be acquired).

•It is the goal of such programs to have students learn about the society (or societies) they live in through dealing with the major social, political, legal, economic, and personal conflicts in that society.

In any significant conflict, many of the key forces in society interact with one another, either in a struggle for dominance or in an attempt to resolve a problem. These forces function actively in society, thereby revealing their real objectives, their actual interests, their real nature and their effective power. This clearly applies to political groups (e.g., the government or the army in some countries), social groups, economic interests, religious forces, ethnic organizations, and so on.

But rather than replace existing disciplines such as history, literature, or science, a public issues program would *supplement* existing courses of study with a values component. This is one way of learning about society, though not the only way. It makes the subject relevant and interesting. And it provides content or factual component, necessary for education.

•The second (related) goal of CPI is to have students learn to deal *rationally* with normative issues as they arise in society and in personal contexts. Without such abilities and skills, it is believed that a person would be powerless, ineffective, and passive. In effect, the realization of this goal entails learning how to reason, analyze, discuss, listen to others, empathize, and decide.

Here the focus is on rational process or procedure. It is largely cognitive but is not limited to the cognitive inasmuch as respect for others, empathy and sensitivity are essential elements in the process. In any event, it is by means of rational process that one resolves moral/value issues and establishes one's moral principles and creed.

Methodology

To realize the goals of the CPI program at least two sorts of factors are needed. First, there must be program materials in which controversial public issues are presented or from which they are derived.[15] For this purpose, a number of books focusing on citizen rights and police powers, foreign investment in Canada, rights of native people, issues of abortion, euthanasia, capital punishment, compulsory sterilization of non-competent individuals, and the right to strike have been developed. However teachers and students were encouraged to develop their own issues from the multitude of sources available in our society.

In addition, a procedure or methodology was needed. The methodology developed in the CPI project, though similar in some respects to that of the Harvard Public Issues project, is radically different in a number of important respects, and is certainly more fully developed as a rational methodology.

Methodological Concepts

Problem or Issues Centered Program. In most instances, CPI programs focus on real problems or genuine social concerns. Students thus deal primarily with issues that interest them and that are socially important. To deal properly with such problems, students must see the issues from the perspectives of the parties involved in the conflict. However, they need not limit themselves to these perspectives and ultimately students must learn to resolve such problems by means of those principles that the students themselves accept.

Case Study Method. To focus on problems or issues, case studies of actual conflicts are presented. In these case studies, the conflicts and sequence of events are described in as balanced and unbiased a way as possible. This involves focussing on the factors contributing to the problem, including the factual background, the perceptions of the conflicting parties, and especially their values and reasoning. As such, case studies serve as a means for drawing out, reflecting upon, and developing normative principles.

A case study method, thus, begins with the concrete, the observable. Because of this, normative principles can always be related to actual happenings and events, as in the many disputes over euthanasia that constantly arise. By using specific cases as reference points, and the frustrating disputes that arise when one begins with abstract principles or a collection of virtues that students had no part in creating, are avoided. Nevertheless general principles can be developed in using the case study method. The major difference is that the case study method *begins* with the experiential, while speculative, nonexperiential approaches begin with abstractions.

Autonomy of Student.   In the final analysis, the position taken in any discussion *must* be that of the student. The judgment thereby made would be the student's and would be derived from his/her calculations, preferences and reasoning. Of course the student may be challenged, may be asked to support his/her position or consider other positions.

But one (e.g., a teacher) *cannot* make a moral decision for another (e.g., a student). For it would then not be the second person's decision. Nor would it be reflected in the spontaneous and free actions of the second person. Making decisions for others is merely manipulation and in a democratic society is unacceptable and counterproductive.

Basically, students learn the process of moral decision-making *only* through participating in the process of moral decision-making. Parroting the principles and perceptions of others is not genuine decision-making.

Models of Deliberation

The Jurisprudential Model is the model of deliberation used in the Harvard Public Issues program by Donald Oliver, James Shaver, and Fred Newmann.[16] This model is essentially a model of justification. According to its advocates, discussing public issues involves using some forms of legal reasoning. Thus, if one takes a position on a specific issue, one is asked first to determine what the principle underlying that position is, and then display the consistency of one's position by considering the implications of the principle. Such a model is useful for *testing* given positions. In using it students can develop a keen sense of reasoning. However this model does not go far enough.

The Strategic Reasoning Model (SRM) was developed to complement the Jurisprudential Model, which is too narrowly legalistic. The SRM is an instrumental model of reasoning with one difference. It incorporates a moral/value component *explicitly*. As such it is a more complete rational model of social deliberation.

This model was developed to provide an account of how courses of action are decided upon, not simply how given positions are justified. For, in moral decision making, "the right-best thing to do" is sought, not only the justification for doing it.

In effect, the intent was to *discover* what to do in a situation, what course of action to take. For in any problem situation, a choice or choices must be made. This entails coming up with alternative courses of action as prospective solutions to the problem. The SRM *reconstructs* the reasoning process an agent goes through. Though it is not meant to be a formula to be followed literally step by step, it does incorporate *all* the relevant *factors* that one must consider in dealing with a problem, if he/she is to reason properly. It is a theoretical reconstruction, not a recipe. For there are no recipes of creative problem solving.

The Strategic Reasoning Model

In all moral decisions (indeed in all normative decisions) the following factors *must* be included. These are the necessary conditions of rational, moral decision making. That these are in fact the elements going into moral decision making, will be illustrated by the examples following the presentation of the model.

•*Goals* [G_i]—The specific goal sought in the context of a broader value system. They specify a given object or state of affairs striven for. Goals are never set up in isolation but form part of a network of values which is not explicitly stated.

•*Relevant Conditions* [G_i]—These form the context in which conflicts arise and are the factors that affect the realization of the goal or goals, either positively or negatively. These include objective facts, how those involved perceive the facts, the goals of other parties in the dispute, etc.

•*Alternative Principled Strategies* [$PS]_1$, [$PS]_2$...[$PS]_n$—These are the competing means-end or strategic principles that the decision maker has come up with. Each of these specifies how effectively and acceptably some means or course of action will be in attaining the desired goal. Generally, these Principled Strategies are expressed as follows:

In situation C, M is an effective, acceptable means for achieving G.

In practice, several principled strategies are listed. It is important to note that such statements are both factual and ethical. That is, a factual causal claim is made about M being effective and a normative ethical claim is made about its being acceptable.

•*Principled Strategy Computation* [PS]—The next step is to choose one strategy from amongst the various alternatives. This requires making a judgment that considers effectiveness (which is determined inductively) and acceptability (which is decided on moral grounds). Somehow a balance must be struck. Since there can be no formula for striking such a balance, it will have to be done intuitively.

•*Decision*—At this point a practical decision to carry out an action based on [PS] is made, The decision maker would state, "I shall do M."

•*Action*—This is the doing of M. Certainly this requires an act of will and knowledge of how to do M. However, in moral education courses students rarely go beyond the judgment or decision.

Examples of Strategic Reasoning

A model of rational decision making is useful only if it can be applied to actual social practice. Unless such a model can somehow express or reflect (a) the essential components of what is recognized as good examples of decision making; (b) the relationship between the components; and (c) the force of the reasoning, a presumption is raised against the model. In looking at a model one may ask: Is this the way people reason adequately? Are there examples of adequate reasoning that does not conform to this model? Is anything else involved? These are important considerations because once we accept something as a valid model of reasoning, it becomes the standard by which reasoning, decision making, and problem solving are judged, both in social/political situations and education.

In fact, I came upon this formulation of Strategic Reasoning from my reading of historical and political works and from reflecting on how colleagues, students, and politicians actually work through problems. Though there are antecedents to this model, and these antecedents may have influenced me, the major determinant of the model came from my perceptions and my experience. In this section, I wish to present a few examples of S.R. that I came across in working out and testing the model.

De Gaulle and a "Free" Quebec

In an explanation of General De Gaulle's call for a free Quebec and his encouragement of French-Canadian separatism in 1967, the political scientist Keith Spicer reconstructs the general's strategic reasoning in the situation. Essentially, Spicer is recounting what some well-informed sources in Paris claim to be the "underlying causes" of De Gaulle's surprising behavior.

> According to these observers, the prime reason for General De Gaulle's ill-humour was Ottawa's stubborn refusal, since about 1963 to sell him uranium without control over its peaceful use. General De Gaulle, so the story goes, only got interested in French Canadians when he thought he might use their resentments as a lever to pry a cheap, long-term uranium contract out of Ottawa—not only for his small, but growing, atomic strike force, but to ensure that France did not miss the boat on uranium as a domestic-energy force as it did with oil in the Nineteen Twenties.[17]

From this account and some background knowledge it is easy to see that De Gaulle's reasoning conformed to the Model of Strategic Reasoning. In a first premise, '[G_1]', the goal sought by De Gaulle is stated. Here, reference is made to the immediate goal of obtaining cheap Canadian uranium with no strings attached. Of course the possession of the uranium would be a means to the larger goals of developing an advanced French technology exploiting nuclear energy for both military and nonmilitary purposes. This in turn would be related to a larger geopolitical role in European and international affairs.

In the second set of premises, '[F_i]' statements of what De Gaulle perceived to be the relevant factors in that context are stated. Among these would be his perceptions of large stocks of high grade uranium in Canada, the weakness of the Canadian Prime Minister, Mr. Pearson, the pressures on Mr. Pearson from the USA, especially from President Johnson, not to sell uranium without controls to France or any nation other than the USA, Canada's instability in having a minority government, the separatist threat to the government, his own influence on the French Canadian population, France's lack of sources for cheap uranium, and so on.

In the third premise, '[PS....]', the crucial principle, on the basis of which De Gaulle decided on his course of action, is presented. Given how he perceived the total situation, De Gaulle would have to decide on the most appropriate, acceptable means or strategy for achieving his goal. Implicit in such choices are general principles that would be applicable in like situations. In this case, De Gaulle could have decided to take a soft approach and considered extracting concessions by holding cultural exchanges, send the Follies Bergères to Montreal, becoming charming and warm towards Mr. Pearson, and so on. This was rejected as ineffective and slow. He could also have tried to threaten Canada with trade sanctions and travel barriers. This too was rejected as too weak. In effect he considered a third strategy of interfering in Canadian politics by exerting pressure in an area of great vulnerability for the federal government by calling out in public "Vive le Québec libre!" This he saw as effective and acceptable in light of Mr. Pearson's perceived weakness. In effect, he rejected the principle of the carrot as too weak for this situation and chose the principle of the stick instead. Unfortunately for himself, De Gaulle underestimated Pearson's character and his decision: "Therefore I shall call for a free Quebec at a public gathering in Quebec city." ([M_1]) evoked Pearson's strong reaction and the cancellation of De Gaulle's visit. For Pearson, De Gaulle's intrusion was politically unacceptable. So in effect, at the core of the differences between the two were differences in values. Nonetheless both leaders reasoned in the same terms of the SRM.

Queen Victoria and the Sparrows

In 1847 the Crystal Palace was completed in London. This magnificent glass structure was seen by Queen Victoria as a major achievement of her reign, the dearest jewel in her crown. Unfortunately, events did not turn out as she planned. Rather than bringing forth crowds of overawed visitors from Britain and abroad enjoying its exhibitions and performances, the Crystal Palace was virtually deserted. It seems that the warmth and light created by the glass structure attracted thousands upon thousands of sparrows. The noise and the dirt resulting from this massive invasion of birds discouraged many of the fastidious would-be visitors who disliked the noise created by the sparrows and shunned having their top hats and bonnets soiled by these intruders.

The Queen was greatly distressed by the turn of events. She sought counsel from architects, builders, planners, and advisers. One suggestion was using buckshot to chase off the birds. But this was unacceptable because it would not have a massive effect on the birds and it would seriously damage the glass structure. A second suggestion was to place chemical drums that exploded at regular intervals in places where the sparrows congregated. However this too was unacceptable because the noise that would temporarily drive away the sparrows would irritate the visitors to the building. Poisoning was also suggested and rejected because of the mess the corpses would create.

Finally, near despair, Queen Victoria summoned the aged Duke of Wellington for advice. After she recounted the problem to her great general and national hero, Wellington paused, then uttered in a crackling voice: "Sparrow hawks!" And this solved the problem—till the structure was destroyed years later.

Once again, from this account, it is evident that all the ingredients of S.R. are present in the complex reasoning underlying the Duke of Wellington's two words. The goal was to have a magnificent structure in which the accomplishments of Imperial Britain would be displayed and in which happy subjects could stroll. Such a structure would enhance the glory of the monarch and the empire. However, the immediate goal, was to rid the Crystal Place of sparrows, which prevented the structure from serving its intended purposes. Such were the values of the Queen, hence Wellington. The relevant factors had to do with the nature of the structure, the sensibilities of the visitors to the Crystal Palace, the physical conditions throughout the structure, the invasion of sparrows. The strategies included direct assaults on the sparrows, annoyance of the sparrows, and so on. But those strategies were neither effective, nor acceptable. Only the military strategy of the Duke worked without compromising the higher goals. It was based on finding an enemy of your enemy who is your friend. The choice of several sparrow hawks was based on such a principle and was certainly effective within acceptable limits. Once the decision to bring sparrow hawks was implemented, the problem of the troublesome sparrows in the Crystal Place was solved.

Montgomery and Rommel

In military situations, especially in the planning of battles, strategic reasoning is especially critical. In such contexts, conflicting, incompatible goals are striven for in the same physical context. Errors in perception and choice of principles can be disastrous.

The risk and complexity of the military situation was conveyed to me with some force in my reading of some of the accounts of the battle of El Alemein, which took place in 1943. As in all conflicts, both political and military, many different plans, thoughts, and reasoning are involved. Some are compatible with others, some are not.

Prior to the battle of El Alemein, Rommel had led the German and Italian forces to two victories over the British forces, one at Tobruk, the other at Benghazi. In both cases he had a strong mechanized force outflank the southern flank of the British army and in so doing inflicted severe losses on the British, forcing them to retreat.

At El Alemein the British, Australian, New Zealand, and other forces had regrouped opposite the German-Italian forces. Rommel had become involved in political difficulties and was recalled to Germany just as the battle was forming. But he had worked out a battle plan.

What is most intriguing in such a situation is its complexity and openness. First of all, there are two sets of goals, the British goal is to vanquish the Germans within "acceptable" British costs and casualties and the German goal is to vanquish the British within "acceptable" German costs and casualties. Both generals, however, consider many of the same relevant physical conditions. These include the terrain, the weather conditions, the number and deployment of their own and the opposing forces, and so on. However each general must also take into account both the perceptions and the planned strategies of his opponent. Thus Rommel, in making his plans would take into account what he believed the British plans and perceptions to be. In turn, Montgomery in making his battle plan studied Rommel's personality, his approach to warfare, his past performances, and so on. He thus made his plan on the basis of what he believed Rommel's plan to be. This required not only constructing a Rommel-type plan but also considering what Rommel thought the British would do, given that the British tried to determine what the Germans would do. The working out of plans and responses could go on indefinitely.

As it turned out, Montgomery's perceptions and plans were the more accurate and this contributed heavily to the British victory. For example, Montgomery correctly anticipated another outflanking attempt by the Germans and set up an ambush in a hilly area to the south to destroy the attacking force when it came to that area. At the same time he attacked what he correctly saw as a vulnerable juncture in the enemy lines where the German forces ended and the Italian force began. Thus Montgomery's decision or problem solving was valid in as much as he had clearly defined goals, a fairly accurate perception of relevant physical and psychological factors, considered various options and applied the principle-based plan or strategy that effectively achieved the planned goals. And of course he carried out the plan. In contrast the German plan failed to anticipate how the British would use the hilly terrain in the south and how the Italian troops would act once they were isolated from the German force. Certainly the British victory and the German defeat at El Alemein were connected to their respective perceptions and reasoning.

Problem Solving in Schools

The foregoing examples all dealt with problems in political and social contexts. Though the actual problems were those confronting monarchs, presidents, prime ministers, and generals, they are similar in form (if not intensity) to the problems confronting people in ordinary life. The same sorts of factors operate in all spheres. Thus the Model of Strategic Reasoning is seen to be an important device for understanding society and functioning in social situations. It is also seen to be an important device in education for the learning of social skills, as the next two examples indicate.

In a film[**] on moral development in education, an actual classroom discussion situation purportedly showing moral reasoning is shown. In a sixth grade class in Tacoma, Washington, the students are presented with a dilemma. Though the responses to the problem lend themselves to an analysis in M.D. terms, they lend themselves equally to an analysis in S.R. terms.

The students are told that they have been given a homework assignment in a science course that involved using a lighted candle. The assignment was due the next day. They were also told that when they arrived home they found a note from their parents that they (i.e. their parents) would be home late, after their bedtime. In the note they were told to do their homework and not stay up late. The students also knew that they were not to light matches or start a fire in the house if no adults were home. What should the student(s) do?

Most of the answers given were rather standard. Some students would do the experiment carefully and explain to their parents how important it was. Others believed that obeying the rule was more important. However one student, in truly creative problem solving fashion said, "Do the experiment outside the house."

**An Introduction to Moral Development* (1977), produced by Dave Bell Associates, Hollywood Ca. Distributed by FILMS INC, Chicago, Ill. Distributed in Canada by Visual Education Centre, Toronto.

In that case, the student exhibited some skill in strategic reasoning. His goals were complex, but included doing homework and obeying rules at home. The relevant factors included the school assignment that involved the starting of a fire, the assignment deadline, the absence of adults, and the prohibition of lighting fires when adults are absent. Various strategies are suggested, with each one somehow incompatible with part of the value system. However the strategy chosen was based on the principle that one should create a new context in which none of the values would be undermined. Thus by going outside, the student could complete the assignment without violating an important rule.

Undoubtedly, one would argue that going outside would create a danger for the child, and *safety* is a crucial value. I agree that on a substantive level the criticism is correct. However it does take considerable rational skill, as the student displayed, to create a situation that would dissolve (hence resolve) the problem. Thus the force of the solution lies in its *formal* (not substantive) insight.

The James Bay Power Project

To illustrate how the SRM can be used to exemplify the decision making process, an actual classroom discussion that took place in an eleventh grade class in 1972 at Westview Collegiate in North York, Ontario will be reconstructed.

In a history course dealing with native people, the class discussed the issue of whether the James Bay Power project[18]
should be implemented in Northwestern Quebec. This discussion took place well before the decision of the Quebec government was taken. In their discussion, the students quickly realized the need to sort out the conflicting goals and values operative in the situation [G_i]. Most agreed that an increase in power output to serve commercial and social needs of North Americans was a worthwhile goal in itself as were the maintaining the natural beauty and ecology of the region and the protection of the rights of native peoples to continue living their traditional forms of life, or choose the form of life they prefer.

In conjunction with this, a range of social, political, economic, technical, cultural, and even personal matters were considered [C_i]. Among these were the physical-geographical conditions (i.e., the five river systems involved the wildlife, forests, etc.), the legal and moral claims of the native people to this area, the life-styles of the natives, the plans to harness the power generated by the five river systems, the anticipated effects of the project on the environment, the role that U.S. power needs played in the making of the plans, the stated and unstated reasons of the Quebec government for carrying out the project, the legal procedures followed, court decisions rendered, future needs of society, and many others. Of course these factors never emerged as distinctly as just stated, but some level of awareness of each existed.

When a general or overall picture developed, (it is *never* complete), various possible strategies in the context—$[PS]_1$, $[PS]_2$, $[PS]_3$—were considered. At one extreme, some students argued that if the original plans for a massive power project were carried out with generous compensation to native people for the loss of their land, the economic and social needs of all Canadians would be best served while the native people would have the opportunity to resettle or readjust under acceptable conditions. And though the beauty of the area would be affected and a few thousand native people would not be able to continue living their traditional way of life, these disadvantages would be minor compared to the advantages. At the other extreme, it was argued that the scrapping of the project entirely would be best because the protection of the rights of native people and the preservation of the beauty of the country and the ecological balance are more important than increased industrialization that would cause greater environmental problems and the profit that only a few people would gain. A compromise was also suggested as a third option in which a reduced project using one or two of the larger rivers would be carried out with some compensation to native people. Under this scheme, a balance between all three goals—economic, aesthetic, ecological, and political—was struck in order to get the greatest benefit with the least disadvantage. In all three cases, a principled strategy in which a program [M] was related to the goals it attempted to approximate, was stated.

At the next stage, the critical computation process of deciding which strategy (hence resulting policy) would achieve the best or most acceptable amalgam of results. Here an affirmation of values by the students become evident. In effect the relative importance of economic prosperity, natural beauty, legal and political rights for each of the students emerged. The consensus in the class was to go for the compromise. Interestingly, this was the approach later taken by the Quebec government.

It must be noted, however, that no situation remains static, and that today, twenty years later, momentum is gathering opposing the completion and expansion of the project. It seems that today that ecological concerns are seen as more important than they were twenty years ago and more important than immediate economic gain. If the value of maintaining the ecological balance predominates in our society, it will lead to a decision of freezing or perhaps curtailing the James Bay power project.

Beyond Possible Reason

The examples presented and analyzed are meant to indicate that there is a common rational way of dealing with social problems. Though there is no recipe for solving all problems, there are factors that have to be established and dealt with according to certain norms. Generally these norms are consistent with one another and ultimately their use carries with it better outcomes. Thus coming up with a fairly consistent system of values is to one's benefit, as would discovering through induction the best means to a desired goal, within that system of values. This is the rationalist's vision and much human progress and many good things in this world can be attributed to such rationality.

But how much faith can we put in rationality? Are there limits to its use? Do rationalists not have expectations that are too high? Are they not seduced by their own rationalism?

Though I always had uneasy feelings about rationality, my first systematic doubts crystallized when I came across hosts of *insoluble* (not merely unsolved) problems. Rationalism was safe as long as I confined my thinking to closed situations that came to a resolution, as in the five examples I just presented *seemed* to be. That is, if you bring thinking to a stop, rational principles work. But things do not simply stop. As a result solutions to problems do not end problems to solutions. Or as an old (unattributed) Irish saying goes, "For every solution we have a problem."

This limitation to rationality came home to me in the late 1970s while reading a newspaper on August 6. I remember the month and, day, though not the year. It was, the anniversary of the bombing of Hiroshima. There was an article in which the rationale for the bombing was presented. It was claimed that 1,000,000 U.S. lives were saved, as well as the lives of many more Japanese, because it made an invasion of mainland Japan unnecessary. Ironically, in another article, it was noted that nuclear weapons, the salvation of 1945, now constituted the major threat to human survival and that billions of people, not only millions, could die in a nuclear war. Thus, it was claimed, even the USA is more vulnerable in the 1970s than in 1945. Perhaps these effects were knowable, perhaps not. But what would a rational person do in 1945? How can we know that what is rational at one time, becomes irrational at another?

The debate over Hiroshima has persisted for many years. Perhaps the irrationality of the bombing *could* have been known at the time. But a perusal of the other front page articles made me wonder. In one article, a Gulf of Mexico oil spill was reported to have destroyed the shrimp industry in Texas, Florida, Louisiana and Mexico. A few years earlier the discovery of oil in Mexico was seen as its economic and social salvation. But we now know that it has resulted in great debt and the same inequitable distribution of wealth, especially in the light of the fluctuation of oil prices and severe damage to the important shrimp-fishing industry. Recently, economic thinking has shifted once more. Instead of relying on an uncertain, diminishing resource like oil, the experts now tell us that we ought to rely on a more rational system of trade. In effect, they say, the salvation of Mexico, the United States, and Canada lies in the creation of a massive free trade zone in North America including these three nations. Any bets?

In another front page article, it was noted that improvements in the design of the Hearn generator in Toronto were causing serious concerns. Ten years earlier the pollution level in sections of Toronto was at a hazardous level due to emissions from the Hearn electrical generator at the city waterfront. In such a case, the rational thing to do is to build a high smoke stack, 700 feet high in fact, to carry the pollutants beyond the city. Unfortunately the acid rain caused by the smoke stack emissions are destroying the lakes and forests in Northern and Central Ontario, as well as fish, fowl, and animal life in these places.

In still another article, it was noted that the wonderful inventions of central heating and central air conditioning are causing enormous wastes in fuel and seriously aggravating the energy crisis that existed at the time (and still exists). Previously, when people heated with fireplaces or small heaters, only the used areas of buildings were heated, thereby conserving fuel. Now all areas of most buildings are heated or cooled day and night, whether in use or not, the result being an enormous waste of precious fuel. But what seems rational when there is a perceived fuel glut seems irrational when there is a perceived shortage.

Since reading that issue of a newspaper, I have focused my attention more and more to the ironies of rational social change. Nowhere are such ironies more evident than in human history and politics. The British victory over the French at the Plains of Abraham in 1759, by removing the French threat to North America made possible the American Revolution of 1776 (which was anathema to those same victorious British), which made possible the French Revolution of 1789, which led to the accession of Napoleon to power, the Napoleonic wars, and the subsequent French disaster at Waterloo in the War of 1812, which made Quebec amenable to Confederation in Canada in 1867, and on and on to the crisis in Quebec in 1970 and to a possible secession of Quebec from Canada by the year 2000. In short we have come a full circle. Victories arising out of rational decisions become defeats and defeats attributed to rationality become victories.

Why does this happen? In general terms, it can be attributed to the limitations of the rational method. More will be said of this in the next section dealing with law and the legal process, the ultimate in rationality. But at this point I will note two reasons for the limitations and frequent failures of rationality.

First, rationality works only in a closed system and social existence is not a closed system. Just as Gödel's world is incompletable and Heisenberg's world is indeterminate, so human social existence is incompletable and indeterminate. As noted in the account of the rational planning of Rommel and Montgomery prior to the battle of El Alemein, whenever two or more individuals are locked in conflict, where the reasoning and perceptions of one's opponent are relevant for a sound decision, the process is incompletable. For each perception becomes a factor that enters into calculation of one side, and the perception of it becomes a factor in the reasoning process *ad infinitum*. Thus the process is incompletable and good results can be no more than momentary. As such, significant outcomes are indeterminate.

A second related "reason" is that the very process of decision making enters into the process it is supposed to deal with. But in entering the process, decision making changes the situation. Because of this, the former basis for choosing a course of action no longer exists. Thus the conditions in which the problem arose, no longer exist. If so the solution therein devised may not be projectable, may not work. Or, if it does, it can be only a matter of luck.

In effect, thinking or reasoning in a situation changes that situation and makes it uncontrollable. Thinking cannot be nailed down. It cannot be objectified. We can no more deal with thinking as a dynamic factor in a situation than a hand can grasp itself grasping, or an eye see itself seeing. In effect, rationality and its processes create the conditions that make its own realization chancy and on occasion, impossible.

As a result, social indeterminacy seems all pervasive. Rationality, institutions, new programs, operative policies, the functioning of mind, and the very process of reasoning where two opposing forces consciously directed tangle, all serve to make planned outcomes unknowable, indeterminate. Thus indeterminacy is not the function of one procedure or one area of social action. It is the function of whatever we do consciously and of the means we use to do it. If so, technology, education, prisons, psychology and social planning are not the effective instruments of enlightened people. And though we cannot imagine society without it, neither is law. It may well be that law, the ultimate in rational control, is least effective in doing what if pretends to do. A detailed consideration of how law and anarchy are so intricately related, now follows.

Notes

1. John Dewey, *How We Think*, 106. Thus, for Dewey, the scientific method was "the only authentic means at our command for getting at the significance of our everyday experiences of the world in which we live" (J. Dewey, *Experience and Education*, 188) [1969])

2. See: J. Bruner, *The Process of Education* 17 ff; E. Fenton, *The New Social Studies*, p. 16ff; A Newell and H.A. Simon, "GPS, A Program That Simulates Human Thought" in E.A. Feigenbaum and J. Feldman (eds.) *Computers and Thought*, p. 279 ff; and for a description of several models of rational problem-solving J.P. Guilford "Frames of Reference for Creative Behavior in the Arts." In J.C. Gowan, J. Khatena and E.P. Torrance, *Creativity: Its Educationally Implications*, (Second Edition) p. 34 ff.

3. *Values and Teaching*, (Columbus: Charles E. Merrill-Publishing Co., 1966) 27.

4. *Ibid.*, 28-30, (lst ed.); 27-29 (2nd ed.).

5. S. Simon, L. Howe and H. Kirschenbaum, *Values Clarification* (New York: Hart Publishing, 1978).

6. *Ibid.*, 39.

7. *Ibid.*, 40.

8. *Ibid.*, 36.

9. H. Kirschenbaum, "In Support of Values Clarification," *Social Education*, May 1977.

10. A series of articles outlining various aspects of Kohlberg's theory are found in L. Kohlberg, *The Philosophy of Moral Development* (New York: Harper and Row, 1981).

11. *Ibid.* See chapter 3, "The Justice Structure of the Prison: A Theory and an Intervention," *The Prison Journal* 51, 2(1972). 1972.

12. See D. Oliver and J. Shaver, *Teaching Public Issues in the High School* and F. Newmann (with D. Oliver), *Clarifying Public Controversy*.

13. See J. Eisenberg and M. Levin (eds.) Canadian Critical Issues Series (General Publishing, OISE Press (1972-80).

14. Mark K. Krug, *History and Social Sciences* (Waltham, Mass.: Blaisdell Publisher) 5.
15. See J. Eisenberg and M. Levin (eds.) Canadian Controversial Issues Series (General Publishing, OISE Press) and P. Bourne and J. Eisenberg. *Social Issues in the Curriculum*, Chap. 2.
16. See D. Oliver and J. Shaver, *Teaching Public Issues in the Secondary Schools*, 114 ff and F. Newmann (with D. Oliver), *Clarifying Public Controversy*, 237 ff.
17. K. Spicer, "The Fictions and Facts of Franco-Canadian Affairs" *The Globe and Mail*, Toronto, 22 August, 1967, 7.
18. J. Eisenberg and H. Troper, *Native Survival* (Toronto: OISE Press, 1973) 1-13.

Part II

The Nature of Law

Introduction to Part II

Three closely related problems were outlined and discussed in the previous section of this book. On first impression they may seem pretty remote from one another. The futility of trying to conceptualize mind, understanding why the stated objectives and the actual operations of institutions are so frequently at odds with one another, and considering ways of dealing with sociomoral problems do not seem at first glance to fit very neatly together. But in my mind they do. For, in each discussion, the naive belief that we can achieve rational control of our destinies is questioned. And in each, the rational upshot of the discussion is to say farewell to twentieth century psychology, education, politics and law, as well as to the seventeenth and eighteenth century epistemology they are based on. But rationality just may not be very rational.

More specifically, in the somewhat speculative introduction, the position is taken that we must come to terms with the fundamental indeterminacy in our personal and social lives. To a great extent, it is asserted, the social world we live in is not rationally controllable, because it is not rationally determinable. For rational method cannot take rational method into consideration in dealing with problems.

This hypothesis is given some support in the next three chapters, which draw primarily from my experiences of failure as an educator and academic, as well as from relevant theories that account for such failures. The first chapter attempts to uncover the basic mistake psychologists make in trying to understand and control social behavior. In viewing mind as a determinable, detectable, indirectly observable entity, these psychologists fail to deal with the fundamental awareness, the active process of creating concepts and world views. If so, it not surprising that control will fail sooner or later.

Unlike the introduction and first chapter, the next two deal with practical, educational, and social matters, with the implementation of programs. At this level, not only do the factors underlying indeterminacy of *knowing* enter, but the factors underlying the indeterminacy of *doing* are suggested. Thus, in these chapters, the social structures needed to bring about change are considered as are the models or paradigms of thought underlying social action.

Specifically, the second chapter focuses on the influence of institutional structure on the moral context of education and by extension on social behavior. It would seem that *how* we organize education permeates in some indeterminable way *what* we learn and what we do. For this (and other reasons), it is impossible to control (or determine) how the organization affects content or curriculum. As a result, the outcomes of moral education programs bear little resemblance to the plans on which they are based. If they do, the similarities can only be attributed to coincidence.

The third chapter goes beyond the institutional structure in moral education to the theories of learning, reasoning, and decision making in the sociomoral realm. Though the various programs discussed present methods for dealing with personal moral problems and social issues, none is really satisfactory. They are riven either with limitations or inconsistencies. Ultimately, it would appear, the rational approach leads to a form of indeterminacy, in the sense that rational decision making models cannot provide the means for solving sociomoral problems in a clear, determinable way. They cannot take into account the use of rational decision making models in solving these problems nor can they take into account the openness or indeterminacy that rationality presupposes. So once again, the use of rationality is at best limited, at worst futile.

At this point, it may be interesting (as well as fruitful) to carry some of these themes to the more general level of civil law. Though law goes beyond specific institutions as schools, prisons, and scientific research labs in its scope of application and concern, and can in extreme cases of totalitarian states apply to all personal and social relationships and activities, many of the same factors and processes that afflict the more limited social programs seem to be involved in spades. Essentially every personal thing we do, from the thoughts we express to the transactions we engage in are, in some respects at least, matters of potential concern for law. Moreover the structure and operation of every social institution is to some extent regulated by law. On every level of existence we are confronted by the specter of law. Law is the second shadow in our lives. (Death is the third.)

The questions now arise: "Does law somehow provide us with the framework and instruments for coping with one another, with our institutions and our environment, rationally and effectively?" Or, "Is law infected with the same indeterminacy as are education and other social forms and practices?"

The remainder of this work will deal with these general questions.

4

Law as a System of Rules

A Bit of Historical and Social Background

In recent years, the role of law in Western society has grown considerably in importance. Not only are there more laws and a greater variety of laws, there is, more significantly, a growing tendency to deal with social conflict and social problems in general, in a formal legalistic manner. This in turn has placed enormous pressure on the legal system to the point where the functioning of the legal system is in jeopardy.

Evidence of this phenomenon is suggested in the statements of high judicial officials reported in newspapers with great frequency. Typical of such statements are the following:

> Chief Justice Warren E. Burger said state and federal court systems could "literally break down before the end of the century" because of the burden of work being placed on them. The U.S. Supreme Court already is so over burdened that it can no longer perform "in keeping with" the standards expected of it.[1]

However the growth of law is not exclusively an American phenomenon but is equally apparent in Canadian society, as the following remarks indicate.

> Federal laws create 97,000 separate offenses while regulations add half a million to the list, Justice Minister Mark MacGuigan told the Canadian Bar Association yesterday.[2]

While Mr. MacGuigan was disturbed by the excessive growth of law, he promised to rectify the situation by reducing the number and character of the offenses, suggesting that somehow he could control the situation. But even reducing the number and character of offenses seems to have had little effect on the problem in the eight years following the speech. Today the situation is far worse and it is clear that the legal system cannot perform the function it is meant to. As court cases accumulate, delays in holding trials grow and as a result more and more charges are dismissed.

> [Attorney-General Howard] Hampton said that in October [1990], after the Supreme Court threw out a series of charges in the Askov case because they had taken too long to come to trial, ministry officials estimated that as many as 150,000 charges could be at risk.[3]

Mr. Hampton is prepared to deal with the problem by appointing many new judges and Crown Attorneys, extending the hours that court facilities are used and withdrawing some of the minor charges. But one may ask, "Is this the way to deal with the crisis in law? Is more law the cure for the illness of law?"

However the growth in law is not always seen as a negative phenomenon, as some supporters of the Canadian Charter of Rights and Freedoms believe. Thus, it is announced in a front page headline in Canada's national newspaper

GROWING BODY OF RULINGS HAS BREATHED LIFE INTO CHARTER.[4]

But regardless of whether the growth of law is a good or bad thing, it appears to be part of a larger trend. One writer sees it as part of long term social and political changes going back to the late thirties and the MacKenzie King government.

> At the outset of the Second World War, Canada had already been transformed into a regulatory state. Reliance on individual responsibility, market forces and minimum policing role for government had given way to state planning and income redistribution. Public policy was increasingly concerned with non-economic issues such as social justice and national unity.[5]

In the United States, the transformation into a regulatory state had been more rapid and intense, especially in the Roosevelt era. As Professor Morton Horowitz of the Harvard Law School noted, common law in all its informality had become the rallying point of reactionaries longing for a preindustrial society long past and was steadily replaced by formal administrative and statutory law.

In short then, the United States, Canada, and all other Western societies have in recent years been moving away from loose, informal modes of dealing with conflict and other problems to more clearly-defined, formal, legal regulation of society. If so, there is considerable warrant for saying we live in a legalistic society.

Increasingly, the notions of law, legal principles, justice, and especially rights find their way into our social vocabulary and profoundly influence our social activities. Within the past fifteen years or so groups have sprung up advocating native rights, nonnative minority rights, women's rights, gay rights, children's rights, animal rights, the rights of victims of crime, the right to life of the fetus, rights of the handicapped, and so on. While such groups base their position on ethical and legal principles, they are engaged primarily in a social/political activity. In effect what they are doing is using the law as an instrument of social change. For law is not only more accessible to more people than in the past, it is increasingly being seen as an effective means of achieving social and political goals. It has become the preferred instrument of rational people in our society.

Even those expressing cynicism about law do not hesitate to try legal means to achieve their ends. Thus radical feminist groups in the United States and elsewhere have lobbied to change rape laws and family law and have campaigned to bring about an equal rights amendment guaranteeing equal wages to women for work of equal value and responsibility. Native groups in Canada have campaigned against the new constitution, have used the courts to press their land claims and even have asked the courts and government to recognize their right to self-determination. Pro- and anti-abortion groups, as well, call for the enactment of laws and use the courts to achieve their conflicting ends. A western Canadian editor who has gone on record as opposing the newly enacted Canadian Bill of Rights, used that Bill as a basis for legal action and won. And most surprisingly, a member of the revolutionary Socialist Workers Party (SWP) who has consistently denounced the government and police in Canada as the illegitimate tools of bourgeois capitalism, sued the Royal Canadian Mounted Police (RCMP) for the violation of his rights following information he received concerning a raid on SWP headquarters by RCMP officers. In such cases, some litigants have succeeded in their endeavors, others have failed and the jury is still out on others. In this case, the SWP litigant (predictably) lost.

In the field of education, this growing legalism can easily be detected. Besides the near-paranoid concern of boards, administrators, and teachers about being sued for malpractice, negligence, invasion of privacy, or any other conceivable tort, school programs and curricula have been changed to meet newly perceived needs and interests. These broad concerns are reflected in the programs offered at teachers' colleges or faculties of education. Where few or no courses in law were offered fifteen years ago, courses in school law, computers and law, business law, and teacher liability are now standard courses in these institutions. However, most impressive is the growing interest in law in secondary schools throughout North America in the past ten years or so. While the development of law programs in United States schools is more intensive and varied than elsewhere, Canada is not too far behind. Half a generation ago, there were virtually no formal courses in law in Ontario. However by the mid 1980s, 65,000 students were enrolled in the Intermediate Law Course, making it one of the most popular elective courses. Possibly, several times that number of students deal with some aspects of law in business courses, life skills programs, family life programs, people and society, people and politics, and history courses. It would seem that most students completing school today have some familiarity with law through their studies. Until recently this held for very few. Perhaps this could account for the growing phenomenon of classroom lawyers that teachers often tell me about, half in humor and half in dread.

The justification for a growing emphasis on legal studies or legal aspects of society would seem to be fairly obvious. In a society, where social solutions are increasingly becoming legal solutions, it is necessary to understand law on two levels. First, it is contended that in order to understand the functioning of society it would be necessary to understand one of its essential ingredients, law. In effect, all social inquiry and social studies presuppose a basic knowledge of law. This is, of course, a matter of educational interest. In addition, it is believed that in order to function effectively in a society whose *modus operandi* is legalistic, it would also be necessary to understand law. This, in contrast, is a matter of social and even political interest.

Support for the presentation of new and better law programs in the schools was expressed in a fairly recent article, where it is stated that in opposition to the commonly held cynicism about law and the legal process

> current trends in secondary school social studies courses may produce a generation of Canadians who realize that a working knowledge of law is essential to understanding Canadian politics, economics and society. Teachers have grasped the importance of legal education, students are keen to pursue it and publishers are preparing learning materials to meet the demands of these new programs.[6]

All the ingredients for this most relevant of theoretical and practical understanding, namely legal understanding, seem to be in place. We need only await the positive results of legal education in the coming years—a crime free society by no later than 2020 A.D.

However a critical question now arises: "What is law?" That is, "What is it that needs to be understood before society can be understood or before one can function effectively in society?" For educators and ostensibly for politicians, two even more critical questions also arise: "Given the nature of law, does one's understanding of it help one function more effectively in society?" Perhaps the ultimate question is: "Is an understanding of the law even possible?"

On the matters raised in these questions, there is considerable difference of opinion. And it is on these matters that I wish to focus in this section. The questions themselves are theoretical in essence. But they do have important practical implications. For one's conception of social education rests on one's answer to these questions as does the way one functions in society. Moreover of broader philosophical interest, the answers to these questions, or more accurately my answers to these questions, will reveal some of the limits of human understanding, especially social understanding.

Hart's Conception of Law

A commonly held view of law today is that it is a system of rules. This view has been carefully and forcefully developed by H.L.A. Hart in his influential work *The Concept of Law*. Briefly, Hart sees law as being made up of two kinds of rules that he calls (a) primary rules and (b) secondary rules.

Primary rules essentially impose obligations and duties on members of society. Very often they take the form of prohibitions, though not necessarily. Thus there are rules that we must pay income tax, not cross streets at red lights, care for children, keep within the speed limit, not rob or assault others, and so on. If we violate such rules we are liable to sanctions or punishment. Thus rule breakers can be admonished, fined, deprived of their liberty, and in some places and times deprived of their lives.

In contrast to primary rules, secondary rules are essentially power granting rules. Such rules endow individuals or groups in society with the authority and powers to carry out their social and legal functions. Thus there are education acts giving authorities the powers to devise and administer the operation of an educational system, police acts endowing determinate individuals with the authority and powers to monitor society in specific ways and to prosecute violators of the law, and a host of laws pertaining to marriage, wills, legislation, and so on. Such rules differ from primary rules in that they are aimed more at facilitating the operation of society than in the control of deviant behavior. The violation of secondary rules, unlike the violation of primary rules, does not as such bring punishment to the agent. It results, rather, in the nullification of an act. For example if a will is not drawn up according to the conditions laid down in law and is not signed or is not witnessed, it is simply not a valid will, hence has no legal force. Similarly, a couple going through a marriage ceremony performed by someone not endowed with the authority and power to marry people will not be legally married. In effect, to facilitate the operation of society, this second type of rule is needed.

Though Hart is frequently quoted as stating "The union of primary and secondary rules is the centre of the legal system" it should be noted that he qualifies this statement with "But it is not the whole."[7] Hart believes that every legal system needs an ultimate rule which he calls "The Rule of Recognition" to endow the total system with validity. Without a commonly accepted rule stating explicitly (or rendering implicitly) that a legal system is *itself* legitimate, the proper authority of the courts, legislature, police, and schools in that system could be challenged. Every group of thugs could then have its own legal system and legitimacy would be no more than the power to enact rules and enforce them. Hart also claims that a genuine legal system does not exist unless society generally accepts and follows the rules that have been properly laid down. If most rules are consistently ignored or violated, regardless of their validity, the legal system has broken down and no longer exists.

From this brief sketch of Hart's conception of law, it is perhaps understandable why it is so widely accepted. It is elegant in its clarity, directness, and simplicity—a rarity in legal writing. Two sorts of rules based on an ultimate rule of recognition form the heart of this view of law. Within this system, the legitimacy of law is explained without an appeal to a fictitious contract or some contrived moral foundation. It goes a long way in accounting for the variety of laws and institutions in our society without straining our credulity.

For the rationalist, this conception is engaging in that it focuses on the rational and civil in human society. As rules, laws become rational means of regulating society and of achieving social goals and ideals. For example, by income tax laws and regulations, the operation of society is funded while wealth is to some degree redistributed, and by the criminal code a basic order in interpersonal activities is achieved. In this scheme, rules become the guideposts that humans follow consciously in determining their deliberate behavior. Members of society are not viewed as passive conditioned objects controlled and manipulated by laws. Rather they are viewed as rational beings capable of voluntary decisions in following or deviating from rules and thereby accepting responsibility for their actions.

On this view the concept of rule is fundamental. Understanding the law as well as functioning under the law require understanding the nature of rules and how they operate. Often, the rule-based nature of the law is clarified by an analogy of law to rules of a game. In so doing, some vague suggestions as to the nature of law as rules and the critical importance of law in human society are made.

The Analogy of the Game

> *A visiting king asked the Caliph, "What is chess?*
> *Responded the Caliph, "What is life?"*
>
> —*Islamic legend*

In this quaint legend,[8] the not uncommon notion that life is like a chess game, or even that life *is* a chess game is expressed. On this view all the key elements of human life are present in a chess game—conscious rational beings, opponents, struggle, conflict, maneuvers, strategies, surprises, benefits, losses, and strict rules. It is the rule-governed action that makes the analogy to life most compelling. For just as the rules of a game control the behavior of the players, so the laws of society control our social behavior.

To try to function in society without knowing the law is like trying to play a game (e.g., chess, hockey, or soccer) without knowing its rules. At the very least such ignorance would severely hinder one's play. More likely it would make play impossible. For, how could one possibly play chess without knowing the rules governing the movement of each piece? How is one to know who is to move first, second, and so on? How would one know *that* the pieces are to be moved? Under such circumstances the only proper moves would be those that happen by coincidence to be compatible with the rules. But given the vast number of possible moves on and off the board, the likelihood of this happening would be infinitesimal.

Even partial ignorance of rules would seriously impair one's ability to play the game. Imagine someone trying to play soccer without knowing the offside rule or the no-hands rule. That person may know that the object of the game is to put the ball in the net as frequently as possible, but he would be frustrated in his endeavors if he disregarded the positioning of his opponents and was constantly offside or used his hands to direct the ball into the net. Once again the likelihood of succeeding in the game would be near zero if one lacked knowledge of the key rules.

Similarly, to function successfully in society, one must know the key rules of society and this in large part requires knowing the essential laws of society. Without such knowledge, the distinction between theft and the purchase of goods could not be made. Working, raising children, educating others, travelling, performing at concerts, carrying out economic transactions, communicating, and a host of other activities would be made difficult, if not impossible. Most human aspirations would not be realizable because one could not know what means for realizing one's aspirations are socially acceptable and what the limits and scope set by society on one's activities are. Even if one chooses to ignore some of the laws of society, as successful criminals and other scoundrels do, one must *know* the laws that one is breaking in order to avoid the sanctions imposed by society. Just as successful athletes know when and how to break rules, so some successful criminals know when and how to break the law. But all such deviants must know what the law is if success is their goal and not conformity or some higher morality. And for those nondeviants who conform to social norms or aspire to a just existence, knowledge of the rules of society is even more crucial.

If this is so, then one of the major tasks of educators today is to educate students in the law, perhaps with a dose of morality to make it respectable. On Hart's view this would mean going beyond the memorization of existing rules—both primary and secondary. It would mean having the students develop an understanding of the nature of rules, the assumptions underlying the existence of rules (i.e., the conditions making rules possible) and most important, the application of rules to relevant situations (i.e., how to apply rules). This would involve distinguishing between rules and empirical laws, between rational actions and natural processes—between doing things for reasons and conforming to the laws of nature. It would involve learning how rules operate, that rules (unlike empirical laws) can be violated and what the relationship between the violation of rules and sanctions is. It would mean learning about the nature of responsibility, of rights and obligations. And much much more. In essence, it would involve learning *about* social rationality, as well as learning social rationality itself.

Criticism

However this view of law (and legal education) is not universally accepted. Some critics of the position argue that although law contains rules, law is much more than a system of rules. Aside from the fact that the so-called Rule of Recognition is a fiction, the operation of law in contemporary Western societies cannot take place with only primary and secondary rules. In his very influential work, *Taking Rights Seriously*,[9] Ronald Dworkin claims that Hart's view of law is much too narrow in that it fails to include the crucial determining role played in legal decisions by such distinctive elements as principles and policies. According to Dworkin, principles and policies are not written rules nor are they formal laws. Yet without them, Western legal systems would not operate as they do.

For example, in a famous American case, *Riggs v. Palmer* (1889)[10] the use of principles in law is clearly demonstrated. In this case, a person convicted of murdering his grandfather sought to claim his inheritance from his grandfather's estate, in accordance with the terms of his grandfather's will. However his application was denied on the basis of an accepted principle in U.S. law that "no one shall profit from his own wrong doings, evil or crimes." In spite of the fact that the rules of inheritance and wills favored the applicant, an unwritten, informal, *moral* principle overrode these rules in the legal decision.

Such principles enunciate moral positions held by society and have considerable force in legal decision-making. A more dramatic example of this appears in Canadian law in events associated with the *Clifford Olsen* Case (1981).[11] Here a suspect in the serial murder of an indeterminate number of children and teenagers was paid $90,000 by the attorney-general's department to reveal the location of the graves of some of his victims. Of significance in this case is that in the mind of the attorney-general of British Columbia (supported by the federal solicitor general) *two* conflicting principles were involved. First, there was the principle used in *Riggs v. Palmer*, that stated that one should not profit from one's crimes. On this principle no payment should be made to a criminal. However there was a second principle, namely, "The suffering of the victims of crime and their families should be minimized." Since the families of the victims of the crime were suffering extreme anguish at not knowing whether their children were dead or alive, it was decided that the suspect would be paid to reveal the location of the graves of his victims. Another factor influencing the attorney-general was that the revealing of the graves by the suspect would help convict the suspect in an otherwise uncertain case, hence payment to the suspect was seen as warranted. Here the principles of minimizing suffering and payment to gain the conviction of a dangerous killer were given precedence over that denying profit from crime.

Another element guiding legal decisions are policies. Unlike principles that are moral in nature, policies enunciate common social interests, hence are *pragmatic* in nature, according to Dworkin. Thus in *Denison Mines v. A.-G. Canada* (1972), [12] the Supreme Court of Canada upheld a prohibition to sell a uranium mining company to U.S. interests by its Canadian owners on the grounds that a government policy to keep vital Canadian resources under the control of Canadian citizens is in the common interest of all Canadians, hence is a valid and relevant consideration in this case.

Repeatedly, in key legal decisions in Canada, the U.S., Great Britain, Australia and elsewhere, principles and polices play significant roles in determining legal judgments. Yet principles and policies are not rules. They are more flexible and quite distinctive in their operation. The major difference, according to Dworkin, is that principles and policies do not have the "all or nothing" (or, as Dworkin calls it the "either/or") quality of rules. One either violates a rule or does not violate it. There is no middle ground. Thus one breaks the no smoking rule in the lab or does not, or one either violates the sixty mph speed limit or not. Moreover, there cannot be contradictory rules in the same system as for example, "Smoking is never allowed in the chemistry lab" and "Smoking is allowed in the northeast corner of the chemistry lab." In any rational world, both of these rules cannot coexist and at least one would have to be dropped or modified.

However principles and policies are not so clear cut and conflicts between competing principles and policies are not unusual. In the Clifford Olsen case, two or three distinct principles seemed to have some relevance for the attorney-general's decision, and it was decided that under the circumstances that the principles relating to the suffering of the families and the obtaining of the conviction were most relevant, and not the principle concerning profit from crime. Similarly governments may have many general policies in a host of areas which come into conflict with one another, as when policies to help farmers conflict with policies to phase out the growing of tobacco and other harmful products. In such cases the courts must decide which policy should take precedence under the circumstances.

There are, as well, other differences between principles and policies and rules. As rules of society, laws are recorded formally in statutes or elsewhere. Principles rarely, if ever, are. This is clearly so in those cases in which a principle is first invoked. Moreover the violation of a rule entails a possible sanction. But no sanction is imposed for violating a principle. Principles and policies are used to determine what counts as acceptable legal behavior and not necessarily to coerce citizens into behaving in specific ways as rules are meant to do. Thus the defendant in *Riggs v. Palmer* was not *punished* in being deprived of his inheritance. Rather, under the circumstances the grandfather's will was invalidated. More so with the Denison Mines case. The mine owner was not punished for violating a law. Rather the proposed sale was judged not to be an acceptable, legal transaction. The upshot of this is that Hart's conception of law is inadequate because it fails to incorporate vital moral and pragmatic elements in the scheme of law.

It would seem that Hart's conception is most plausible in its characterization of law in its more or less normal application, as when a known rule is applied to a clearly relevant case. However it is deficient when a law is limited for the first time in its application or when a case is not clearly covered by a given rule or law. This deficiency becomes more apparent in a close examination of the analogy between rules of games and laws. Though rules of games and laws bear important similarities to one another in that both define what acts are prohibited, what acts are permissible, who may do what and when they may do it, and when penalties are to be applied, critical differences also exist and the analogy breaks down.

For the rules of any *existing* game are *static*. The rules of chess, hockey, or tiddlywinks are fixed. They operate throughout a game, tournament, or season. One cannot change the fixed rule governing the movement of pawns in mid-game or mid-tournament, nor can one institute a new offside rule in overtime. A possible exception to this took place in the 1985 world chess championship tournament between Anatoly Karpov and Gary Kasparov. In this event the president of the international chess federation cancelled the tournament when the current champion Karpov appeared to be in danger of losing his title, although he was ahead five games to three at the time. Many observers cried "Foul!" and criticized the president for his arbitrary action. It appeared to these critics that a new rule had been introduced at a critical point in the tournament and this was considered not to be "cricket."

In contrast, laws in a legal system may be dynamic, as well as static. Laws constantly change and new grounds for reaching verdicts or judgments established. Many instances of this have occurred in recent years. Laws relating to war crimes have been made retroactive though rules against retroactive legislation existed. In 1988, a suspected war criminal was indicted in Canada on the basis of retroactive legislation, in a country where the alleged crimes did *not* take place. Similarly with the development of new technologies, such as computers, new concepts of privacy and property arise. In effect, there exists in society a dynamic process of development wherein rules themselves are invalidated, modified, changed. Old rules no longer apply to the new conditions and are rejected. New rules evolve, are accepted on the basis of newly recognized principles arising in newly emerging conditions, and are applied to previous actions. This process of change or development of law is an essential feature of contemporary Western law. For there to be such change, there must be elements and mechanisms other than rules that make the change in rules possible. More than a fictitious super-rule or ultimate rule is needed, for this too may be subject to change.

Law is, therefore, much more than a body of specific rules. It differs from rules of a game. While they are in operation, games are sealed off, so to speak, from the impulses of the rule makers. Whereas, law *qua* legal system is a process tied to social, technological, political, and economic forces. Factors enter into the process that are distinct from the actual rules. One such factor is the value system of society, as in the Riggs and Olsen cases. Another factor may be political or economic concerns as in the Denison mines case.

Laws do not arise in a vacuum. They arise in response to perceptions, needs, social goals, material conditions. They arise in the unfolding of events. They form part of history. As part of the process of history, the legal system has a dual existence. On the one hand it is influenced by social and other forces. On the other, it influences human behavior and social organization. It determines, yet in turn is determined. It is not merely a product, nor is it above society. It is everchanging.

The issue of whether law is essentially a product or a process is in some respects analogous to a critical issue in the philosophy of science. According to Richard Rudner,[13] two different notions of science exist. On one view, science is a corpus of statements derived according to the rules of scientific method. Among these statements may be definitions of terms, assumptions, axioms and findings, including the laws of nature, hypotheses, and theories. As such, science becomes a product. The central focus is on the facts derived in science, that is, its scientific findings. In opposition to this view, it is held that science is essentially a search, a striving. Whatever products or findings result from the search constantly change, are superseded, leaving only the process of search as a constant. The corpus of scientific findings vary from age to age, whereas only the process of search remains.

As we have seen, law may be similarly viewed in two different ways. It may be viewed as a body of rules, the product of a system itself governed by rules. Law may also be viewed as a process or an activity generating, among other things, rules. As such law is essentially dynamic and changing.

Whether one conceives of law as a set of determinate rules or as a dynamic process is, however, more than a matter of academic interest. Lawyers who see law as a static system of set rules will operate within the existing framework of rules and interpretations much as the person doing normal science in T.S. Kuhn's *The Structure of Scientific Revolutions*.[14] In contrast, lawyers who see law as a dynamic process, will more likely challenge existing regulations and concepts, much as the revolutionary scientist in Kuhn's work. Some of the most important changes in law have been the result of challenges to existing laws. In the *Drybones* case,[15] G.B. Purdy, a young lawyer fresh out of law school challenged the validity of a section of the Indian Act that imposed harsher punishment on Indians convicted of drunkenness than the criminal code imposed on all other persons. On the basis of the earlier, somewhat vague Bill of Rights, which had never been applied before (or since) in any Supreme Court decision, the appeal of the accused was upheld and a section of the Indian Act invalidated by the Court.

On several occasions, convictions for Strict Liability Offenses (i.e., offenses for which the performance of an act is sufficient for conviction and for which no defence is acceptable) were overturned. In the *Jollimore* Case, [16] the conviction of a person accused of driving without a valid license was overturned because he had not been informed that his license had been revoked. Prior to that decision, no reason would have been acceptable. Similarly in the *Rees* Case,[17] the conviction of a man for having sexual relations with a sixteen-year-old girl was overturned because he could not have possibly known under the circumstances that the girl was under the legal age of consent. Once again the defense used in the appeal would not have been accepted previously.

In all these cases, important changes were made in the law because broad principles of justice or fairness or equitability, beyond specific statutes and regulations, could be appealed to. If so, it would seem that one's conception of law has in critical instances significant practical implications. One may view law as a system of set rules or one may view it as a dynamic process. However the former view of law cannot account for the nature and scope of changes in law in Western society.

Notes

1. *The Nation, The New York Times*, 7 Nov. 1983, 2.
2. *The Globe and Mail*, Toronto, 30 August 1983, 1.
3. *The Globe and Mail*, Toronto, 27 March, 1991, A10.
4. Kirk Markin, "The cutting edge of the law," *The Globe and Mail*, Toronto, 13 April 1987, 1.
5. Dominique Clift, "Balancing rule of law in a world of regulation", *The Globe and Mail*, Toronto, 31 October 1983, 7.
6. Paul Hornbeck, "Doing Justice to Legal Education," *Quill and Quire*, 46,5 (May 1980), 4.
7. H.L.A. Hart, *The Concept of Law* (Oxford: Oxford University Press), 96.
8. Salem Alaton, "The Pawn Brokers," *The Globe and Mail*, Toronto, 26 June 1982, 3, Fanfare section.
9. Ronald Dworkin, *Taking Rights Seriously*, (Cambridge, Mass: Harvard University Press, 1977).
10. 115 N.Y. 506, 22 N.E. 190 (1889).
11. *R. v. Olsen, Dominion Law Report*, 1981.
12. *DLR*, December 19, 1972 (S.C.O.).
13. Richard Rudner, *The Philosophy of the Social Sciences* (Englewood Cliffs, N.J.: Prentice Hall, 1966) 1-3.
14. T.S. Kuhn, *The Structure of Scientific Revolutions*, (Chicago: Phoenix Books, 1966), 23-34.
15. *Drybones v. R, DLR*, 1968.
16. *Jollimore v. R*, N.B. (1963)
17. *Rees v. R.*, B.C. (1972).

5

Law as a Historical Process

Afterthought: Law as Essentially Rules?

It may be possible to see law as a complex system of rules without denying that there is a process of law that is historical, social, political, and perhaps ethical in nature. On this view, the rules or laws of the system constitute the substance of law, that is, after all, what people living in society are primarily concerned about. This is not to deny that law arises in a social-historical context and that such developments constitute the process of law. According to the straw man I have just erected, interest in the process of law would primarily be found amongst academics—historians, sociologists, philosophers, and the like. But such a process would be at least once removed from the functioning legal sphere, wherein social activity is regulated formally by the state.

However, I cannot accept this view either, because it does not account for changes in law as it operates. Rather it describes what laws are (prohibitions, obligations, etc.), how humans and corporate units administer laws and society, and why the system is acceptable or legitimate. What it fails to mention is how the functioning and development of the system constitute, hence affect, the system. This level of operation is not, as stated above, one level removed from the operation of the law but is rather an integral part of law. If so, to understand law adequately would first require understanding the operation and development of law, not only its components or substance or rules in the abstract. Moreover, if one's effective operation in society is dependent on an adequate knowledge of law at all its levels one would have to understand the process of law at all its levels to operate effectively in a sociolegal system or state. If physicists cannot ignore the process they are involved in, why should lawyers and other subjects be able to do so?

Two Supporting Experiences

For me personally, the differences in the sort of understanding involved between the two notions of law, that is, between law as rule or product and law as historical-social process, were brought home dramatically while observing the reactions of a number of very different groups of students attending court sessions. Somehow the myth has been perpetrated in educational circles that one of the best ways for students to learn about our justice system and at the same time appreciate its great social value, is to observe court proceedings and see justice in operation. If only it were that simple. Quite the contrary in fact occurs and my experience has been that such visits to court mostly breed cynicism. Students seem less impressed by the wisdom and iron logic of the judge than by the fact that there is a clear pattern of discrimination in the system.

Two examples should illustrate my point.

As do many secondary school classes in Ontario and probably everywhere else on earth, an eleventh-grade History and social studies class from George Harvey Secondary School spent a morning session in Magistrate's Court in order to see first hand how the justice system works. The students came from mainly working-class families in a mixed urban, commercial, and industrial section of metropolitan Toronto. Most of the students were the children of immigrants and came from a variety of ethnic backgrounds, though the largest single group came from a rural or small-town Italian background. In general, the group members were lively, argumentative, and practical in their concerns. Most planned to learn trades or crafts, but a significant number wanted to study engineering or law, and one or two even wanted to study literature or music at university.

In the court session that they attended, nine cases were tried. The charges ranged from assault and battery to petty theft and breaking and entering. All but one of the accused appeared to be under twenty years of age. The exception was a well-dressed burly man who appeared to be in his early thirties. He was charged with assault.

In six of the nine cases there were convictions and jail sentences. All six convicted were young, shabbily dressed, confused, and hardly had any defence. Most pleaded guilty and may not have had lawyers acting on their behalf. A seventh accused failed to appear and a bench warrant was issued for his arrest.

The man charged with assault denied all charges against him in an aggressive, confident manner. Throughout the proceedings he glowered menacingly at the accuser who testified against him and he quite categorically denied the allegation that he even touched his accuser. The alleged victim stammered throughout his testimony. In the end the accused was acquitted of all charges.

The ninth accused was a well-dressed youth, represented by a well-known lawyer and supported by his parents, the only ones present in court. Though he had a record of convictions for theft against him, he was not sent to jail but given a suspended sentence and ordered to undergo psychiatric treatment.

After the court session the Court Clerk spoke briefly to the class about the court and "our" system of justice, without making any reference to the cases tried. He then asked the students for their impressions of the proceedings and was taken aback by the comments he received. Among the comments were: "It's all Mickey Mouse!", "The guys with the suits get off!", and "You didn't find out what really happened!" In this last comment, the reference was to the assault case on which they had no doubts that the accused was guilty and the witness intimidated. The next day, in class, the students were even more vocal in their criticism of the criminal justice system. Being young and poor, they felt they would be "taken" by the system and never given a fair trial, if they stood accused before the courts.

In a second instance, a similar impression was registered by graduate students at the Ontario Institute for Studies in Education who had attended court proceedings. As part of an assignment in a values education practicum, I suggest that the students examine functioning institutions to determine whether the practices of these institutions are consistent with their stated ideals or objectives. Every year one group decides to examine the Court system. Every year the reactions of the group are similar. Typical, were the experiences of a group that attended a session at night court in Toronto dealing with traffic offenses.

As in the previous example, a clear pattern emerged. Five recent immigrants who spoke English with difficulty and who came without counsel were all convicted as charged and fined accordingly. Three teenagers were also convicted and fined, although they denied the police officer's testimony, in part. Five of seven more mature, well-dressed men who were fluent in English were either not convicted (three cases) or had their fines reduced (two cases).

In their presentation to the values education seminar, the members of the group concluded that the practices of the court favor the affluent, adult, nonimmigrant population. It favors those who by virtue of their status in society not only know the law and its practices, but also know how to beat the system, which involves knowing how to plead, how to dress, what to say or not say. Thus, the group claimed, the court system is inconsistent with the ideals of justice and fairness that such moral philosophers as Kohlberg and Rawls have taken great pains to define and recommend.

So, in effect, both student groups reacted in a similar manner to the court proceedings, in spite of significant differences in age, education, and social position. Senior school administrators saw eye to eye with the sons and daughters of bricklayers. One sixteen-year-old student, of working-class immigrant background said, "The law works for the powerful against the weak," while a chairman of a history department said, "The legal system is biased against the poor, the young, and the non-English-speaking immigrant." Both groups concluded that the legal system was unjust, as practiced.

But how valid are the arguments of these students? How adequate is their analysis of the system? Are their harsh judgments justified? Though I clearly do not wish to be seen as an apologist for a flawed legal system, I find the reasoning of both groups to be somewhat narrow and far from persuasive. One of the reasons why the students were cynical is that they saw only one dimension of law.

All they saw were rules applied to cases. Thus an eighteen year old charged with stealing a transistor is convicted and jailed on the evidence of the security officer of the store and a thirty-three-year-old Portuguese immigrant is convicted and fined for driving eighty mph in a fifty mph zone on the evidence of a police officer using a radar device. In both cases, individuals were convicted of offenses they committed. In contrast, a thirty-two old salesman is acquitted of assault because of "inconclusive evidence" resulting from conflicting testimony. However, apart from the merits of the individual cases, imperfections in the broader legal system became evident when the law consistently punishes the poor, the young, or the newly arrived non-English speaker and allows the wealthier and other members of society to slip through the legal net. This they saw as unfair.

What they did not see was the larger process of law in which change and occasionally development are possible. It is one thing to see a court case as a contemporary social phenomenon that is biased and unfair to certain groups. It is something quite different to see that case in the context of historical developments over a period of time. The former view derives from seeing the case or cases as relatively static, and self-contained, whereas the latter derives from seeing the case or cases as parts of a larger dynamic process and as getting their meanings and significance from that process. It is my view that a broader perspective than that taken by the students would have some influence on their conceptions of and attitudes toward law. However, it must be stressed that broader perspectives in themselves do not render the unjust just, nor the painful sweet.

To provide a sense of this broader perspective—of law as historical process—I will briefly trace the development of the status of women in marriage and in society in British and Canadian Law from 1718 to the present. Other case studies could as well be used to illustrate the historical nature of the legal process. For example, the development of law related to custody of children, the development of tort law regarding responsibility and liability for damages, or the development of law pertaining to human rights and state power could equally serve to demonstrate the crucial historical dimension of law and the legal process. Surprisingly (to me at least), developments in these areas are by no means uniform or parallel. The developments in family law have generally been positive in the sense of establishing more equitable (though *not* fully equitable) relationships and rights within the family. Developments in tort law are somewhat mixed and there is some confusion as to which principles are most basic in assigning liability for damages. However in the development of human rights legislation, despite all the political rhetoric about the sanctity of the individual and "our democratic system," it would seem that the state is appropriating more and more power to itself while the individual is becoming more and more restricted in her/his real choices. Perhaps this is the price we pay for advanced technology. Whatever the case may be, the emergence of law in all areas is an historical process. And the nature and value of the law in any area depend on a long term process not in specific cases in a short span of time. Any understanding of law *must* include an understanding of that long-term process.

In this work, I have chosen to trace the development of the status of women in the family because the law in this area is at a further state of resolution than the others and a discernible pattern of progress is evident. This in turn allows for a tidier analysis and better serves to illustrate what the legal process is and how it is to be understood than would a case study involving a multitude of ambiguities and uncertain directions. There is something to be said for tidiness and progress in the illustration of a contentious theoretical position, I believe.

A Note on Method Used

The method I will use is to trace a series of key cases and legislation dealing with the same issue or legal concept in chronological sequence in order to determine what rules are operative at successive times, what changes are affected by decisions (especially where precedents are established) and what the underlying principles justifying the changes are.

In some respects this method is similar to that used by E.H. Levi in *An Introduction to Legal Reasoning*. In this work Levi argues against what he terms "the pretense that law is a system of known rules applied by a judge."[1] According to the "pretense," legal reasoning is deductive reasoning and proceeds from Law to Case to Verdict. For example, on a simple theft case a judge is supposed to reason as follows:

1. Law—Whosoever wilfully and deliberately appropriates the property of another, without that persons consent, is guilty of theft.

2. Case—Jones wilfully and deliberated appropriated a radio which is the property of Smith from Smith's residence without Smith's consent.

3. Verdict—Therefore Jones is guilty of the theft of Smith's radio.

As neat and simple as this model is, it does not accurately represent the manner in which the most significant legal reasoning proceeds. For not only is law comprised of "certain, unchanging rules," it is also "uncertain [and] changing." As such it is an open system in which development over time takes place. To make such a development possible, law includes "the mechanism for a moving classification system."[2]

The alternative to the traditional deductive Law/Case/Verdict model is a form of analogical reasoning. Levi asserts that

> The basic pattern of legal reasoning is reasoning by example. It is reasoning from case to case. It is a three-step process described by the doctrine of precedent in which a proposition descriptive of the first case is made into a rule of law and then applied to a similar situation. The steps are these: (1) similarity is seen between cases; (2) next the rule of law inherent in the first case is announced; (3) then the rule of law is made applicable to the second case.[3]

For Levi, however, the process of legal reasoning cannot be fully depicted by an abstract model of analogical reasoning. For such reasoning itself takes place in a concrete historical context, one in which the need for new categories arise and in which old categories break down. Thus Levi sees legal concepts and principles as arising in a determinate three stage cyclical process. This process is depicted as follows:

> The first stage is the creation of the legal concept which is built up as cases are compared. The period is one in which the court fumbles for a phrase. The second stage is the period when the concept is more or less fixed, although reasoning by example continues to classify items inside and outside the concept. The third stage is the breakdown of the concept, as reasoning by example has moved so far ahead as to make it clear that the suggestive influence of the word [i.e., concept] is no longer desired.[4]

Levi illustrates how his models apply in case, statutory and constitutional law. In the section on case law, using a sequence of court decisions from Britain and the U.S.A., he shows how the "inherently dangerous rule" in cases involving third party liability developed from the clumsy attempt in *Dixon v. Bell*[5] (1816) in which a loaded gun given to a servant girl is termed "as by this want of care left in a state capable of doing mischief"[6] to the fairly specific definition and classification of articles as "inherently dangerous" in *Thomas v. Winchester* (1852)[7] to the breakdown of the concept in 1916 in *McPherson v. Buick*[8] when "inherently dangerous" gave way to "imminently dangerous when defective."[9] In effect, then, legal concepts do not remain frozen, but develop over time from case to case as new principles are invoked and articulated. The realm of law is not frozen or static. It is dynamic, always emerging.

The strength of Levi's position lies in its ability to deal with flexibility and openness. He rejects logical models that proceed from fixed general rules to necessary, undeniable verdicts. Instead he opts for a system that relies in part on the insights and ingenuity (and more frequently the lack thereof) of human beings, of jurists, and on the actual sequence of cases. There is a connectedness in his system that emerges from case following case and case building upon case. Far from there being an inevitable outcome in the evolution of legal concepts and principles, there is a prior uncertainty in which the specific details of individual cases, the thinking of the judges as well as the particular sequence of cases influence the determination of principles and rules of law. To a great extent, Levi characterizes law as it "really" operates.

However, I do not follow Levi's approach completely, for in philosophy as in law, no approach is ever complete and final, even those allowing for openness and change. Specifically, I find limitations both in Levi's conception of legal reasoning (i.e., his logical model) and in his conception of the process of development (i.e., his related historical model). Though the model of analogical reasoning applies in a vague way to some legal developments, it does not apply to all developments, certainly not to clear cut cases. When Jones is adjudged guilty of theft, it is *not* because his actions were similar to those of Brown three hundred years earlier in which the modern concept of theft emerged. For his actions to be considered as theft they simply have to meet certain criteria and this does not require their being similar to anything else. Moreover there is more than one way (i.e., reasoning analogically) to derive a precedent or come up with a precedent-making decision. As will become apparent in the coming case study, such precedents are sometimes set on the basis of moral principles that have become newly accepted in society. In such cases finding similarities with accepted conceptions or precedent cases is not essential. Finally I find Levi's historical model overly rational. Levi's focus is entirely on the logic of classification—of how objects are classified in the abstract, of which objects are seen as similar to which objects. What Levi fails to mention is that the concept of "inherently dangerous objects" arose in a period of great industrial and imperial expansion in both Britain and the U.S. It was a period of social upheaval and great political change, of changing conceptions of children and human beings. It was an age in which new power groups in society emerged, in which the franchise was broadened to include not only aristocrats and gentry, but the emerging commercial classes, the working classes, and eventually women. It was the age of the Reform Bills, the Chartists, classical socialist theory, the Married Women's Property Act. It was an age of great economic and technological expansion. In such an age the crippling harm created by the new technology had to be controlled and this was seen to require precise definitions of liability not vague conceptions such as "left in a state capable of doing mischief." In effect, law had to adapt to the new conditions in society. It had to adapt to new driving forces in society.

Unfortunately Levi gives no indication of the influence of the new material conditions and changing world views or philosophical conceptions in society on law. Levi's focus is narrowly on the logic of decision making, especially on the method of changing legal classifications or legal categories. While, it may not be necessary to present an account of social, political and intellectual developments in the nineteenth century to illustrate the nature of legal reasoning, the existence of a relationship between historical factors and legal reasoning must be indicated in any adequate theory or model of legal reasoning. Similarly, I do not think it necessary to reconstruct history in detail to present a view of what law is. However, I *do* think that it is necessary to indicate (however generally) that the unfolding of the process of law does (and must) take place in a sociohistorical context. Legal decisions are never made in the abstract but in the context of political, technological, economic, and social developments.

Case Study: The Status of Women in Marriage

On the most direct and explicit level, my basic interest in this case study is to discern the pattern of development of the status of women in Canada, specifically in marriage, but also generally in society. The cases used were chosen because they appear to have marked some change or significant development in law. Other cases (as well as formal legislation) may have been equally important but it is difficult to determine precisely which intellectual idea or expression or social perception influenced another and especially which ideas led to critical legal decisions. However in this case study, I have chosen cases that appear to be representative of a legal stance, are recognized as being important in law, are frequently cited in other key decisions and are in some instances widely viewed as significant precedents. In all these cases, the legal principles underlying the stance taken are clearly expressed, and a definite pattern emerges.

As noted earlier in this chapter, other cases and other patterns could possibly have been used. However the cases I have selected most clearly reflect the basic conflict of the past two hundred years or so between (a) a Natural Law position in law and society recognizing an interrelated natural order that is rationally determinable and controllable and that follows from self-evident first principles and (b) Humanism that recognizes the central role of human consciousness and decisions on the nature, meaning, order, and unfolding of the world. Not all legal decisions, even today, reflect the same outcome of the struggle underlying all the conflicts of our age, and not all the decisions draw the compromise between the two extreme world views in the same place. However the following case study delineates one instance where the development has been more and more towards a humanistic position, which views law more as social convention than as a part of a natural order. And such an historical development is clearly significant in determining the meaning of individual decisions or groups of decisions, over and above how they are analyzed in their own terms—as when students (or concerned citizens) observe court cases and are appalled by the decisions.

To inquire into long-term historical developments in Canadian law, one must go back to British antecedents. I begin with the Atwood case because its verdict embodies a conception of marriage and womanhood that is representative of one extreme in British law. Because of the clear position it enunciates, this case is referred to in a number of important subsequent decisions.

Atwood v. Atwood (1718)

After receiving prolonged cruel and abusive treatment by her husband, Mrs. Atwood left home. She was tracked down by her husband, forced to return to his home and confined. A writ of habeas corpus was drawn up by her family in order to free her from confinement. In rejecting the writ, the Court of Queen's bench declared the following principle:

> [a husband] has by law a right to the custody of [his wife], and may, if he think fit confine her, but he must not imprison her.[10]

Between 1718 and 1840 this principle fairly well defined the legal relationship between husband and wife as part of the natural order. In effect the law recognized near absolute dominion of the husband over the wife as part of the natural order. Short of taking her life or imprisoning her, a husband was hardly accountable to anyone for his treatment of his wife, hence could abuse and confine her as any other chattel. The main recourse a woman had was to have a writ of habeas corpus issued on her behalf to claim illegal confinement but this rarely succeeded. Or she could apply to an ecclesiastical court run by the church for formal separation, or divorce in those extreme cases where she was imprisoned. But this was not easily granted.

Even as late as the eighteenth century, canon law introduced after the Norman conquest of Britain in 1066 was still very much in place in Britain. Pronouncements of St. Paul that "the head of the woman is the man," "[a man] is the image and glory of God; but the woman is the glory of the man," and especially "Wives, submit yourselves unto your own husbands, as unto the Lord. For the husband is the head of the wife" had taken on legal force.[11] It is clearly reflected in the writings of Sir William Blackstone the most highly esteemed British legal theorist of the eighteenth century who proclaimed that in marriage the wife's person became consolidated with and subservient to her husband's.[12] In spite of Blackstone's plea that we respect and revere mothers, a married English woman in the eighteenth and much of the nineteenth century had no independent legal being. She was not a legal person because nature dictated otherwise.

To our modern sensibilities, the most outrageous results of this legal conception of the natural rights of men and women appeared in those cases where women sought custody or visitation rights to their children after marital separation. In many such cases the absoluteness of the father's common law right to custody against the mother's claim is unequivocally reconfirmed. An often cited case illustrates this.

Rex v. De Manneville (1804)

The De Mannevilles were married in England in 1800. Mr. De Manneville was a French citizen, hence an enemy alien during the Napoleonic wars of that period. Mrs. De Manneville was English. Earlier that year Mrs. De Manneville had left her husband because of alleged mistreatment. She kept an infant daughter who was nursing at the time with her. In her affidavit she claimed that

> On the night of the 10th of April last 1804 the defendant found means by force and stratagem to get into the house where she was, and has forcibly taken the child then at the breast and carried it away almost naked in inclement weather; with a view, as the mother apprehended of taking it out of the kingdom.[13]

In his judgment Lord Ellenborough cited the accepted dictum of Lord Mansfield in 1781 that "the court could not at any age take a child from the father." Then Ellenborough added, "The father of a child is entitled to the custody of it, though an infant at the breast of its mother." However, "[i]f he abuse that right to the detriment of the child, the Court will protect the child. But there is no pretence that the child has been injured."

It is significant to note that the court would act against the father if the child were injured or malnourished, that is, if harm came her way. But no concept of the positive interests of the child was expressed in the judgment. The major concern of the court was that the father would take the child to France, outside its jurisdiction. But since it had no grounds to believe that this would happen, no action was taken and the rights of the father, enemy alien or not, were respected. For paternal rights, took precedence over citizenship in the existing order of things.

Rex v. Greenhill (1836)

A similar judgment to the De Manneville one in that it denied legal status to the mother and ignored the positive interests of the child was given in *Rex v. Greenhill*. What emerged in this case is that a double standard was clearly recognized by the courts. For while any woman having an adulterous relationship would have been considered unfit to live with, let alone have custody of her children, the same did not hold for men.

Though Benjamin Cuffe Greenhill was living with a Mrs. Chambers whilst married to Mrs. Greenhill, he was granted absolute custody of his three daughters.

Chief Justice Denman expressed the position of all four judges when he wrote in his judgment the following:

> There is, no doubt that, when a father has the custody of his children, he is not to be deprived of it except under particular circumstances; and these do not occur in this case; for although misconduct is imputed to Mr. Greenhill, there is nothing proved against him which has ever been held sufficient ground for removing children from their father.[14]

It would seem that an inferior status in marriage not only carries a lack of rights or legal power with it, it also carries greater consequences for sin. Conversely, superior status and power carried with it the right to sin as well. Given the slow move to democracy in the first Reform Bill, it is not surprising that the Greenhill verdict gave rise to a public outcry and to sympathy for Mrs. Greenhill. This response in turn was a factor in the passing of Talfourd's Act (1839) in which mothers were given the right to custody and access to their children up to the age of seven. But there was still the old catch. In order to gain the power of custody and access to their children of tender age, mothers had to be "chaste and unadulterous." This restriction did not apply to fathers. One can speculate that new concepts of the child and maternal rights were beginning to seep into British law. However the basic principles governing the status of women in marriage and society were still overwhelmingly patriarchal and religious (i.e. natural law) principles. This is apparent in the famous Cochrane case.

Re Cochrane (1840)

Alexander and Cecilia Maria Cochrane were married in 1833, with the consent of Mrs. Cochrane's mother. Mr. Cochrane was thirty-two years old, Mrs. Cochrane was twenty-six. They lived together until 1836, during which time they had two children. The elder died, the younger, a son, survived. In May 1836, Mrs.Cochrane left her husband without his consent or knowledge. She, her mother, and her son went to Paris. Between 1836 and 1840 the only communication Mr. Cochrane received from his wife were a few letters from abroad.

Four years later, Mr. Cochrane, by the use of a stratagem (i.e., by a promise of money), succeeded in getting Mrs. Cochrane to his apartment in London. When Mrs. Cochrane attempted to leave, Mr. Cochrane restrained her from doing so and continued to confine her in his apartment. A writ of habeas corpus was then issued at the request of Mrs. Cochrane's mother, by the Court of Queen's Bench "to produce the body of Mrs. Cecilia Maria Cochrane." After hearing petitions from both sides, the Court ruled in Mr. Cochrane's favor, citing in support of its judgment the principle enunciated in *Atwood v. Atwood* that a husband has custody of his wife and may confine her if he sees fit.

However, the court's judgment did suggest a very slight shift when it added:

> When a wife absents herself from her husband on account of no misconduct on his part and he afterwards by stratagem obtains possession of her person, and she declares her intention of leaving him again, whenever she can, he has a right to restrain her of her liberty, until she is willing to return to a performance of her conjugal duty.

Mr. Justice Coleridge justified the court's decision as follows:

> For the happiness and honour of both parties it [i.e., the law] places the wife under the guardianship of her husband, and entitles him for the sake of both, to protect her from the danger of unrestrained intercourse with the world, by enforcing cohabitation and common residence.[15]

He then added that there is greater good in ensuring the stability of marriage than its instability. Therefore it is permissible to sacrifice the happiness of a few for the greater happiness of society. And with a flourish he concluded, "Let her be restored to Mr. Cochrane."

In summary, several matters should be noted. The language used in reference to Mrs. Cochrane is language appropriate for material objects or chattels, not human beings. She is viewed simply as a means to a greater social good, the greater happiness of society. Her own personal aspirations and her right to choose her own goals are ignored. She is seen as a social object not as an autonomous human being. The significance of her existence and her role in society are seen in terms of a natural world order in which all active roles are relegated to males. And undoubtedly there is a theological justification for this world view, in which Mrs. Cochrane has no significant, human role.

Surprisingly, the Court drew on the greatest happiness principle, often associated with utilitarianism to justify its decision, yet utilitarians, and most notably J.S. Mill, were often in the forefront of the advocates of human rights. Somehow, in keeping with their world view, the Court construed justice, rights, and happiness as being compatible (only) with male domination.

But most significant is the reference to the fact that the husband was guilty of no misconduct against his wife. This may suggest a difference from the Atwood case and that a husband's abusive conduct may be relevant to the Court's decision. But such nuances did not change the fact that many women continued to live in dread in unhappy and dangerous marital situations and nothing could be done to alleviate their condition. But times were beginning to change—just beginning.

Ex Parte Sandilands (1852)

Shortly thereafter, the growing recognition of the autonomy of adult women (albeit a severely restricted autonomy) was revealed in the Sandilands case. In 1852, Mrs. Sandilands left the home of her husband to stay at the residence of her son, Mr. Leggatt. Mr. Sandilands applied for a writ of habeas corpus to bring up the body of his wife. In his suit he asked for the restoration of conjugal rights, claiming that Mr. Leggatt had exerted undue influence on his mother to leave Mr. Sandilands.

The Court of Queen's Bench rejected Mr. Sandilands' claim that undue influence was exerted on Mrs. Sandilands. It also rejected his writ of habeas corpus.

> Where a wife is voluntarily and without any restraint absent from her husband, a court of common law has no jurisdiction upon his application to issue a writ of habeas corpus to bring up her body.[16]

Most significant in the court's judgment was the fact that a married women could not be seen as the property of her husband in the same way as children could. Lord Campbell, C.J., in his judgment, spelled out the distinction.

> The case of an infant is quite different, because there the parent has the right to the custody of the child, and if the infant is of tender years the Court will order it delivered to its father. But a husband has no such right at common law to the custody of his wife.[17]

Effectively, this decision served to prevent the Cochrane case from turning into a hunting license for runaway wives. The court system and the police force would not be involved in restoring to their husbands the growing number of wives who were disappearing into the large cities (and elsewhere) of the growing industrial society. This had the effect, as Lord Campbell's declaration indicated, of enabling wives to make some choices previously denied them. However a wife was still basically considered to be the chattel of her husband and Ecclesiastical Courts could still be used to force her to return to her husband "if she has no good cause for being absent from him."

As in every period of great social change and upheaval, there were conflicts between forces of nearly every conceivable sort in the nineteenth century. There were conflicts of economic classes, political groups inside and outside of these classes, artistic schools, religion and science, ideologies, world views, the urban and rural, the modern and the classical and so on.[18] The outcomes of such conflicts never emerge clearly and consistently, hence periods of change as Marx, Kuhn, and most others tell us are characterized by inconsistencies or so-called "contradictions." So it was in the nineteenth century that the change of the status of women in marriage from chattel without rights toward autonomy and responsibility was not consistently in any given direction and often conflicting official legal positions existed at the same time. On the one hand, a growing body of legislation giving wives more autonomy and rights was emerging, while at the same time retrograde court decisions were made at the highest level.

The passage of Talfourd's Act in 1839 initiated a series of legislation that granted women increased rights in the area of family law in Britain, Canada, and the Empire. In 1855 legislation was passed in Upper Canada (i.e., Ontario) granting mothers the right of custody of and access to children up to the age of twelve. As in Talfourd's Act only those women who were chaste and had not committed adultery qualified for these rights. This trend continued in Britain, where in 1873 mothers were given custody and access rights to children up to the age of sixteen.

In 1877, a major breakthrough in family law occurred in Ontario where the Guardianship Act permitted mothers to be appointed joint guardians of their children upon the death of their husbands. Women were also permitted to appoint testamentary guardians of their children in the case of their deaths. However all such appointments required court approval. It was not until 1886 in Britain and 1887 in Ontario that guardianship *rights* were given to mothers. By making guardianship a *right*, a court approval was not necessary and under clear-cut unambiguous conditions, mothers became the official guardians of their children when fathers died. In effect, it is now recognized that a general pattern of the grounds for making decisions in child custody cases has emerged in Canada from the early nineteenth century. Until the middle of the century, the father's right to custody was absolute. For the next fifty years or so, the mother's rights were increasingly recognized. Thereafter to the present the welfare of the child was said to be the primary factor on which custody was decided.

However, one of the major legislative breakthroughs in the attainment of a fully human status by women under the law was the passage of The Married Women's Property Act (1882). For the first time, women were given the right to own property after marriage, thus were recognized as persons under the law in a limited way. Prior to this legislation the husband had by law virtual control over the property and person of his wife. Even the inheritance of a woman was legally under the control of her husband. But with this act, the absoluteness of patriarchal power in the family was undermined.

But even with increased recognition of the guardianship rights of women in marriage and the economic rights of women under the law, major court decisions reflected an adherence to the old patriarchal model of family authority. Two famous cases reveal how entrenched were the old modes of thinking in law despite the emergence of post-reform bill industrialism.

Besant v. Wood (1878)

One of the saddest cases in which the custody of children was at issue had to do with the personal trials of Annie Besant, an early advocate of the social and political rights of women.[19]

Reverend Frank Besant, Vicar of Sibsey, Lincolnshire and Annie Wood were married in 1867. A son, Arthur Besant, was born in 1869, a daughter, Mabel Emily Besant, was born in 1870. In 1873, after a tumultuous and disharmonious marital relationship, a separation was agreed upon because Mrs. Besant embraced atheistic opinions. In a formal deed of separation, Mrs. Besant was given custody of the daughter for eleven months a year and the son stayed with Rev. Besant for eleven months. Each parent saw the other child one month a year.

Then in 1877, Mrs. Besant began publishing antireligious books. No court action arose from these. But, she was indicted for publishing a book *Fruits of Philosophy* in which birth control methods to check the increase in world population were described and recommended. It was noted at the trial that a "jury found that the book was calculated to deprave the public morals." However no charges of immoral personal conduct were levelled at Mrs. Besant.

In his suit, Rev. Besant sought to regain full custody of both children, with no right to access to the mother, because of her publication of obscene materials and for refusing to provide her daughter with religious education. The court found in Rev. Besant's favor and in spite of the earlier agreement, he was granted complete custody of the children and Mrs. Besant was prevented from seeing them again. For, as Jessel, M.R. wrote in his judgment,

> It is the duty of the court to see that a fatherless ward is brought up in the religion of the father.

This would clearly hold for a child *with* a father.

Later that year, 1879, Mrs. Besant sued her husband for restitution of conjugal rights. She did this to be able to see her children. However the court rejected her suit, even though it was likely that a male filing a similar suit at that time would be successful. Moreover the morality of the wife was a condition of custody, which clearly went beyond being chaste and not being adulterous. Morality involved having socially acceptable thoughts and religious views. For failing on both counts, Annie Besant was deprived of the company and companionship of her children.

There was an outcry against the judgment on the part of academics and other intellectuals, including the philosopher John Stuart Mill. Though such protests may have influenced legislation expanding women's rights or even later judgments, they had no effect on some major current judgments in which traditional thinking was firmly entrenched.

In re Agar-Ellis (1883)

The Agar-Ellis case[20] is especially important because it served to test the scope and limits of newly acquired custodial and access rights of mothers. In this case the mother's rights to her children, the desires of children and the welfare of children were pitted against the absolute natural rights of fathers. The judgment starkly revealed what the real powers in society and the operative principles of society were at that time.

Hon. Leopold Agar-Ellis married the Hon. Harriet Stoner in 1864. He was a Protestant, she a Roman Catholic. Prior to the marriage Mr. Agar-Ellis agreed that any children of the marriage be raised in the religion of their mother. Mrs. Agar-Ellis bore four children. After the birth of the first child Mr. Agar-Ellis changed his mind about having the children raised as Roman Catholics. The eldest child died and Mrs. Agar-Ellis secretly raised the three surviving children as Roman Catholics.

In 1878 the Agar-Ellis's separated and Mrs. Agar-Ellis took the children. After one visit that year with his children, Mr. Agar-Ellis, according to his testimony in court, claimed that Mrs. Agar-Ellis "so indoctrinated the. children with Roman Catholic views that ultimately, they refused to go with their father to a Protestant place of worship." Thereupon the father took custody of the children, agreed to one visit a month by the mother with her children and had all correspondence between mother and children read by himself or by a third party. Then in a legal suit he took action to make his children wards of the court, to have their Roman Catholic education cease, and to have them raised as Protestants. The court ruled in Mr. Agar-Ellis's favor and restrained the mother from taking the children to confession or places of worship without their father's consent. Vice-Chancellor Malins ruled that the father could decide which religion his children would be educated in, though he did not stipulate what, specifically, it should be.

Then in 1883 the second daughter, Harriet Agar-Ellis, aged sixteen, petitioned for right of free exercise of religion. Her father agreed and the daughter subsequently practiced Roman Catholicism exclusively. But later that year, while her governess was abroad, Harriet petitioned for the right to spend two months with her mother. She claimed that at age sixteen she had the right to move about freely. However the father opposed this on grounds that he had the right of custody until she was twenty-one years of age and that a two month stay would enable the mother to prejudice her daughter against her father. Harriet's petition was denied by Pearson, M.J.

> on the ground that in the absence of any suggested fault on the part of the father, the court has no jurisdiction to interfere with the legal right of the father to control the custody and education of his children and to decide where they should reside.

At the Appeal Court hearing the following year Mrs. Agar-Ellis and her daughter argued that after the age of sixteen, a person has the right to choose freely where he will go. The appeal also failed and the legal grounds of its failure were expressed in the clearest of terms by three eminent jurists.

Brett, M.R. (later Lord Esher) stated,

> the law of England is that the father has the control over the person, education and conduct of his children until they are twenty-one years of age.

Throughout his judgment, Brett referred constantly to the *natural* affection of the father, his *natural* duties and of course his *natural* rights. Thus he argued,

> The law recognizes the rights of the father because it recognizes the natural duties of the father.

The court could interfere with paternal custody of children in cases where the father is guilty of (1) gross moral turpitude, (2) abdicating parental authority (e.g., exercising authority unreasonably or inconsistently); and (3) intending to remove the child from the court's jurisdiction without permission. Although Brett indicated that he disagreed with Mr. Agar-Ellis's reasoning for preventing mother and daughter from staying together, he recognized the father's authority in this matter because the father was not erratic in his approach. Thus Harriet was prohibited from visiting her mother, primarily because that is the way nature ordains it.

Lord Cotton, as well, had personal difficulty in endorsing Mr. Agar-Ellis's view.

> I can hardly conceive circumstances where a daughter should not have the opportunity of visiting and corresponding with her mother. I should think that would, almost as an unexceptional rule, be of the greatest possible advantage to the infant. But the father takes a different view of the case, and the question

we have to consider is whether the court ought to interfere with the discretion of the father and to say what it would think best for the infant.

The question was a profound and disturbing one under the circumstances. When, if ever, should paternal judgment and authority be overridden? Cotton resolves his difficulty by taking a position commonly taken by all natural law positions, namely that paternal authority, discretion, and rights are in the public good and for the well-being of the child, Cotton wrote,

It has been said that we ought to consider the interest of the [child]. Undoubtedly. But this Court holds this principle—that when, by birth, a child is subject to a father, it is for the general interest of families, and for the general interest of children, and really for the interest of the particular infant that the Court should not, except in very extreme cases, interfere with the discretion of the father, but leave to him the responsibility of exercising that power which *nature has given him* [my emphasis] by the birth of the child.

Once again nature impels us to respect paternal decisions. It is for the good of us all.

Finally, a third opinion of the Court is consistent with the other two and relies, as well, on nature and natural law for justification. Lord Justice Bowen was also peeved at the way Mr. Agar-Ellis has exercised his parental right. But he did not let his personal views interfere with his legal judgment.

the Court must not be tempted to interfere with the natural order and course of family life, the very basis of which is the authority of the father, except it be in special cases

Bowen then clarifies the relationship between his personal judgment of the well-being of the child and his legal judgment.

It is not the benefit of the infant as conceived by the court [members], but it must be the benefit of the infant having regard to *the natural law* [my emphasis] which points out that the father knows far better as a rule what is good for his children than a Court of Justice can.

So in spite of what reason may tell us in particular cases, reason tells us in general that father knows best. Thus Bowen concludes that "the father has an authority which never ought to be slighted."

In conclusion, then, it is easy to see why the Agar-Ellis case can be considered to be so significant. In this one case (or series of actions) issues of the maternal rights to the custody of children, to access to children, to decide on the religious and moral education of children as well as the right of the child prior to its twenty-first birthday to choose its domicile, arise. And on all these matters, the paternal right to determine what happens is considered sacrosanct. What is significant is that in 1884, with the growing recognition of the rights of mothers to access, custody, guardianship, even personal property, a high court can render such rights virtually nonexistent, at least in those instances where paternal opposition exists. But what is even more astounding is that an archaic form of paternalistic natural law founded on the belief in the mystical power of the male seed should be given such legal force and that the strivings for a universal human dignity manifested in reform bills, revolutionary rhetoric, chartist actions, romanticism, and a host of other social activities in the nineteenth century be so systematically suppressed.

The Queen v. Jackson (1891)

Though the language of Agar-Ellis was unambiguous and forceful in maintaining the near-absolute dominance of paternal rights and the unshakable entrenchment of natural law as the foundation of civil law, paternalism, and natural law were not as redoubtable as they appeared. Only seven years after the Agar-Ellis decision, the most radical change in the legal nature of the marital relationship took place on 19 March 1891 when the British Court of Appeals heard *The Queen v. Jackson*.[21]

Edmund Houghton Jackson and Emma Maude Jackson were married in England in 1887. Within a week of the marriage, Mr. Jackson left England to settle in New Zealand and was to be joined by Mrs. Jackson shortly. In the meantime she went to reside with her sisters and brother-in-law. During that time she changed her mind about migrating and asked Mr. Jackson to return to England, which he did. When he arrived, she refused to resume living with him. He sent her letters asking her to return to him, but received no reply. Finally, he sued for and received a decree for the restitution of conjugal rights. On the advice of her sisters and brother-in-law she refused to obey it.

On Sunday 8 March 1891, the decree was presented to Mrs. Jackson as she was leaving church in Clitheroe. Thereupon her husband and two young men (one, a solicitor's articled clerk) seized her, and using only "that force necessary," pushed her into a carriage. In full view of the congregation, she tried in vain to cling to her sister, shouting for help all the while. Finally, she was deposited into the carriage and taken to her husband's house in Blackburn. In the course of the struggle, she received a bruised arm. However, once in her husband's home, she had free run of the house, was attended by a nurse and Mr. Jackson's sister and had a medical doctor available. She was, however, restrained from leaving the house.

At first, police were prepared to charge Mrs. Jackson's sister with assault, but withdrew from doing so. A writ of habeas corpus was drawn up by Mrs. Jackson's family and was heard by the Court of Appeals. In its decision, the Court upheld Mrs. Jackson's right to leave her husband.

The Court's decision clearly broke new ground. Lord Halsbury, L.C., in his judgment, denied "the absolute dominion of a husband over his wife."[22] He saw Mr. Jackson's case as being based on the proposition

> that it is the right of the husband, where his wife has wilfully absented herself from him, to seize the person of his wife by force and detain her in his house until she shall be willing to restore to him his conjugal rights.

Then he added,

> I am *not* prepared to assent to such a proposition. The husband has no such authority as he claims; no English subject has such a right of his own motion to imprison another English subject, whether his wife or anyone else of full age.[23]

Meanwhile Lord Esher, M.R., formerly the Brett, M.R. who justified the absolute natural authority of the husband in Agar-Ellis, now joined Lord Halsbury by saying that if the propositions supporting Mr. Jackson's case were true it would "make an English wife the slave, the abject slave of the husband."[24] He too rejected the absolute or any dominion of the husband over the person of the wife.

What is fascinating in this case is the use of humanistic language. Where previously the language of nature was used—"natural duties," "natural affection," "natural right," "natural law,"—now much more humane terminology appeared. Thus in commenting on the abduction of Mrs. Jackson outside the church Lord Halsbury wrote:

> I confess to regarding with something like indignation the statement of facts in this case, and the absence of the delicacy and *respect* [my emphasis] due to a wife whom the husband has sworn to *cherish* [my emphasis] and protect.[25]

Elsewhere he talks about "common feelings of humanity" in rejecting antiquated laws permitting chastisement of wives.[26] And throughout their judgments both Halsbury and Brett allude to the dignity owed Mrs. Jackson as a mature, adult person.

The Jackson case marked one of the major turning points in family law, not only in Britain but in Canada and elsewhere where British principles and precedents were frequently followed. No longer could a husband with the support of the law claim physical custody of his wife. About half a century *after* slavery had been abolished in British possessions, marital slavery was finally abolished. The principles enunciated in Atwood and Cochrane were dead! In effect, the law recognized that wives were not chattels. And *because* of this judgment, a new and more equal husband-wife relationship was established. The horrible abductions of the seventeenth, eighteenth and nineteenth centuries were no longer legitimized by the Court.

Historically, it is important to note that the actual change in the formal legal relationship between husband and wife can be dated and the principles underlying stated. This is so because law in its various forms has the force of changing social realities *in its statement*. By pronouncing "It is a criminal offense to do X" the law creates the criminal offense X, and by stating in a High Court judgment "A wife is not her husband's (or anyone else's) chattel" a wife's status is established and a change brought about. But more will be said of this in the next section.

The Continuing Historical Process

Today in Canadian, British, and much Western law, the effects of the Jackson decision are still being felt. Very briefly I wish to point out several of the more important judgments influenced by the Jackson decision.

The Women's Suffrage Bills (1917, 1918)

The recognition of the growing independence of the woman in marriage is clearly related to the growing recognition of the political rights of women. For the granting of custody, guardianship and access rights to women were based on a formal, legal recognition by the state of the personhood, or more accurately, the humanity of women in some areas of family life. Similarly the recognition in *The Queen v. Jackson* of the right of a wife to leave her husband, take up residence wherever she chooses and to fulfill or not fulfill her "conjugal duties" as she chooses is a further recognition of her autonomous human status in other areas of family life. And the granting of property rights to wives in The Married Women's Property Act further extended the autonomy of women in economic realms. It would seem evident then, that the Jackson decision together with other legislative and court decisions led directly to the passage of the Women's Suffrage Bill in 1917 in the House of Commons and in 1918 in the House of Lords. By this act, 8,000,000 British women were given the vote. To a great extent the passage of the bill was due to the political activities of women and a few men over a century or more and was precipitated by the activities of the suffragettes. It was also the consequence of new social economic and political realities. However implicit in the bill is a new concept of women, as somewhat (though not yet completely) autonomous human beings in the political realm—a concept related to the concepts enunciated in the Jackson case and the earlier legislation. At this stage, the recognized rights were quite basic, but their attainment was part of a long, complex process. Though autonomy may be an either/or condition in that one is either autonomous or not, the recognition of autonomy has occurred in a piecemeal fashion, from realm to realm, and even then was not granted in full measure. For even in political, marital, and economic realms limitations existed and still exist.

The Persons Case (1929)

The emerging humanistic concept is also evident in the final judgment in the famous *Persons Case* of 1929 which directly affected the political status of women in Canada. After a prolonged court battle in which the Supreme Court of Canada turned down a bid to have women become eligible for appointment to the Senate of Canada on the grounds that women were *not* persons "for right and privilege" though they were recognized as persons for other respects (e.g., child custody), five Alberta women, Emily Murphy, Herrietta Edwards, Irene Parlby, Nellie McClung, and Louise McKinney appealed to the Privy Council in Great Britain. This step was the culmination of a long, frustrating struggle that began in 1916 when Emily Murphy's right to become a police magistrate was challenged. In their decision, the Privy Council concluded that

> Their lordships are of the opinion that the word "persons" in Section 24 [of the British North America Act of 1867] does include women and that women are eligible to be summoned to and become members of the Senate of Canada.

By way of supporting the decision, Lord Sankey commented on the practice of excluding women from public office, then added a curious legal explanation of the phenomenon.

> The exclusion of women from all public offices is a relic of days more barbarous than ours, but it must be remembered that the necessity of the times often *forced* [my emphasis] on man customs which in later years were not necessary.[27]

The Privy Council seemed to recognize that times were changing and that we were entering a more civilized and less barbarous age in which the recognition of the political humanity of women was a necessary condition of civility.

Murdoch v. Murdoch (1973), (1977)

One of the most celebrated cases in recent Canadian family law is the Murdoch case, in which the wife, Irene Murdoch, claimed the right to a share of the property acquired in the family during marriage. At the first trial in 1973, the Supreme Court of Canada rejected Mrs. Murdoch's claim that she was part owner of her husband's farm which was worth over $300,000 and on which she had done most of the work during twenty-five years of marriage. The majority opinion written by Judson, J. agreed with earlier judgments that

> in the absence of some financial contribution, the wife is [*not*] entitled to a proprietary interest from the mere fact of marriage and cohabitation and the fact that the property in question is the matrimonial home.[28]

It rejected the minority opinion written by Laskin, J. that a constructive trust exists between husband and wife and

> As is pointed out by Scott, *Law of Trusts*, 3rd ed., vol. 5 (1965) at p. 3215... a constructive trust is imposed where a person holding title to property is subject to an equitable duty to convey it to another on the ground that he would be injustly [sic] enriched if he were permitted to retain it.[29]

As a result Mrs. Murdoch was awarded only $200 a month alimony but had to pay $2,500 in court costs. However four years later, the Supreme court, in reversing itself, awarded Mrs. Murdoch 25 percent of the joint property. In so doing it recognized the existence of a constructive trust in marriage and thereby denied the husband the right to exploit the wife. For the first time the wife was recognized as an economic partner in marriage. This new relationship was formally decreed in such legislation as The Family Law Reform Act, 1978, of Ontario (and similar legislation in other provinces and other countries) in which "marriage is seen as a union of economic equals" in addition to being a domestic relationship.

Rathwell v. Rathwell (1978)

The following year in *Rathwell v. Rathwell* (1978) the Supreme Court of Canada ruled that a wife is entitled to half the property acquired in her husband's name during their marriage. In this case Mrs. Rathwell had made significant contributions to the farm economy through her labors and financial support.

In his majority opinion, Dickson, J. wrote,

> Many factors, legal and non-legal have emerged to modify the position of earlier days. Among these factors are a more enlightened attitude towards the status of women, altered life-styles, dynamic socio-economic changes. Increasingly, the work of a woman in the management of the home and rearing of the children as wife and mother is recognized as an economic contribution to the family unit....The custom by which real estate was taken in the name of the husband, coupled with the reverence paid to registered title, militated against wives.[30]

Mr. Justice Dickson also noted that the Murdoch decision denying that a wife's labor was a contribution to the family assets is at variance with constructive trust as a means of rectifying injustice. Thus it would seem that in its decision the Supreme Court extended the recognition of a married woman's equal status to include the right to jointly acquired possessions during marriage.

Pettkus v. Becker (1980)

However, the Supreme Court of Canada's decision in the Pettkus v. Becker case may be the most far reaching in defining the economic status of women in that it extends the basic principles of equity and autonomy for women beyond the marital to all conjugal relations. Rosa Becker and Lothar Pettkus lived in a common-law relationship for nineteen years during which time Miss Becker worked alongside Mr. Pettkus in a bee-keeping business, that was registered in Mr. Pettkus's name. She also contributed financially in various ways, such as selling honey door-to-door and using money earned by babysitting, for their joint existence. When the relationship finally terminated in 1974, the farm and business were worth an estimated $300,000. Thereupon Miss Becker commenced an action "seeking a declaration of entitlement to one-half interest in the lands and a share in the bee-keeping business."[31]

In awarding Miss Becker one-half interest in the farm and business, the Supreme Court extended the concept of economic equals to include common law relationships. Dickson, J. in presenting the majority position wrote,

> I see no reason for any distinction, in dividing property and assets, between marital relationships and those more informal relationships which subsist for a lengthy period. This was not an economic partnership nor a mere business relationship, nor a casual encounter. Mr. Pettkus and Miss Becker lived as man and wife for almost twenty years. Their lives and their economic well-being were fully integrated.[32]

As in the Murdoch and Rathwell cases the principle of constructive trust was used to justify equitable sharing of economic assets in marriage. But in this case, unlike the first Murdoch case, the majority of the court accepted the principle as being applicable to the conditions. In quoting with approval from the Rathwell case Mr. Justice Dickson reiterated,

> The constructive trust, as so envisaged, comprehends the imposition of trust machinery by the court in order to achieve a result consonant with good conscience. As a matter of principle the court will not allow any man unjustly to appropriate to himself the value earned by the labours of another.[33]

In effect the Court has ruled that the status of a woman in any conjugal relationship is one that carries with it equitable treatment, that is, a status involving the respect that is due to any human being as a human being. The decision is a rejection of the traditional view that because of some natural order in which women are the weaker vessels, they are denied the same domestic, social, political, and economic status as men.

It is still too early to know how far this new principle will extend or what it will cover. One may wonder whether constructive trust can be applied to all human relationships, including employer-employee relationships, and what "unjust enrichment" will be defined as in future court decisions. In any event, we have come a long way from the Atwood decision of 1718 to the Becker decision of 1980. It has been a long, slow, and laborious process from viewing wives as property to viewing women as equal economic partners in conjugal associations and as having equal rights in politics. However, lest we become self-satisfied over these developments we should not forget the discrepancies between theory and practice and that gross injustices still exist. One has only to reflect on the tragic aftermath of the Becker case. In early November 1986, six years after her "landmark victory" (as the press called it), Rosa Becker committed suicide at the home of her employer where she worked as a domestic. Miss Becker had become extremely despondent at not being able to receive any of the money due to her. Even after her death one last indignity was heaped on the strivings of this brave and plucky woman when on 26 May 1989 final payment of $13,000, all that remained of her share of the joint property, was given to the estate of Rosa Becker.

Despite such unforeseen failures of the law to ensure equity, the thinking of the courts continues to go in the direction of a humanistic view of society and the rejection of a natural law view. This became apparent in the Supreme Court of Canada decision on the appeals of Susan Brooks, Patricia Allen, and Patricia Dixon.[34] The three women in this case were denied unemployment insurance benefits on the grounds that they were pregnant at the time that they made their claims. Previously, the Court of Queen's Bench and the Manitoba Court of Appeals ruled against their claim on the basis of a 1978 Supreme Court judgment that held that women who were discriminated against because they were biologically disadvantaged were not discriminated against because they were women. In effect, accepting disadvantages due to strictly natural phenomena were not discriminatory in the way that discrimination on the basis of sex is. The former is legally acceptable, the latter is not.

However, eleven years later Chief Justice Brian Dickson, who had written the 1978 judgment reversed himself, rejecting his own earlier reasoning:

> Pregnancy discrimination is a form of sex discrimination simply because of the basic biological fact that only women have the capacity to become pregnant.[35]

Since sex discrimination is unacceptable, then the Court ruled the women were entitled to receive unemployment insurance benefits for seventeen weeks of their pregnancy.

Mr. Justice Dickson also wrote,

> It is difficult to accept the view that the inequality to which [other women were previously subjected] was created by nature and therefore there was no discrimination.[36]

In stating this, I believe, Mr. Dickson has essentially rejected any shred of Natural Law in our legal system. For what nature is, seems to have no relevance for social morality, hence law. For law is what humans determine in accordance with human-social values. This became evident when he wrote,

> The better view [than to see nature as the culprit in discrimination] is that inequality was created by legislation.[37]

It is significant, I believe, that within eleven years, so radical a change can occur in the thinking of the same individual, admittedly a most brilliant and unusual person.

The Charter of Rights and Freedoms

A clear indication that women are formally recognized by law as having equal status with men in marriage and all other social, economic, and political realms is found in some of the key passages of The Charter of Rights and Freedoms enacted by the federal government with unanimous support of the provincial governments in Canada.

In Section 15 of the charter, it is stated,

> (1) Every individual is equal before and under the law and has the right to equal protection and equal benefit of the law without discrimination and, in particular, without discrimination based on race, national or ethnic origin, colour, religion, *sex* [my emphasis], age or mental or physical disability.
>
> (2) Subsection (1) does not preclude any law, program or activity that has as its object the ameliorization of conditions of disadvantaged individuals or groups, including those that are disadvantaged because of sex .[38]

By the way of explanation, the following statement appears in the unofficial commentary on the Charter in a government guide book.

> For the first time in Canadian history, the Constitution will make it clear that, for women, equality is not a right to be acquired, but a state that exists. It will ensure that women are entitled to full equality in law—and not just in laws themselves but in the administration of law as well.[39]

One my well object that the Pettkus-Becker case shows that the law cannot *ensure* just administration of law in spite of its statement of entitlement of full equality. Thus it is clear that equality is not and cannot be a state. It can only be a right.

An even more forceful statement of women's equality is made in Section 28 of the Charter.

> Notwithstanding anything in the Charter, the rights and freedoms referred to in it are guaranteed equally to male and female persons.[40]

The force of this "guarantee" is underscored in the accompanying comment which states

> This is one guarantee that *cannot* be overridden [sic] by a legislature or Parliament.[41]

On this view, the law proposes, but it cannot dispose! or *can* it? Perhaps the ghost of Rosa Becker will ask the framers of the charter, why it believes the law can *guarantee* anything.

Summary Remarks

By way of summarizing the view that law is more adequately understood as an historical process than as simply a system of rules applied to cases, I shall list, and in some instances briefly discuss, the key features of such a process. The historical process of law is complex and varied and not completely understood. For the purposes of this work, I will not enter into the problems, but wish only to characterize the process in a very general way.

1. There is a continuity in law. Principles and general outlooks develop in a sequence of related cases over time and a general pattern of decisions emerge. In the cases considered, there has been a development towards greater equality of women in Western society. Through the law, women were granted more rights in marriage and society, more power to make fundamental human decisions and greater authority in many of the roles they performed. But legal developments are not always so positive as they were in family law and the pattern may reveal moral regression, as when the power of the state is at issue.

2. Law is not a self-contained nor independent process. Change always takes place in a specific context and this truism also holds for legal change. This change is not merely a matter of legislators coming up

with new rules or judges with new principles. For law is not simply an abstract intellectual process. More than ideas determine laws. As Dickson, J. wrote in his judgment in the Rathwell case," many factors, legal and non-legal have emerged to modify the (court's) position of earlier days."[42] Such factors as socioeconomic changes, new social attitudes and values and different life styles may affect legal judgments.

3. The most difficult, yet important, task of anyone inquiring into the process of law is to *explain* the process. Thus the critical "question of questions" is, "Why do laws change?" Or put differently, "How can one *explain* the process of legal change?" Such questions relate to a highly general level of law and evoke general, abstract responses. But regarding the sequence of cases and the legal issues presented here, we may ask more specific, less general questions. "Why did the legal status of women in the family and society change in the nineteenth and twentieth centuries?" Perhaps from specific explanations of legal changes, general explanations of legal change may emerge.

4. The answer to the foregoing questions is both complex and difficult. And though I am not clear on the specific reasons for the changes, I can suggest some of the kinds of factors that enter. These factors form part of the context in which specific legal changes occur. The following are some plausible factors.

(a) Changing Social Conditions—In general, as social conditions change, legal rules change. As wealth is redistributed, new social forces arise and society is restructured. Thus in the two "world wars" of the twentieth century, manpower was required urgently in North America and Europe to produce war materials and to fight the war. As a result, in the U.S., blacks and women moved into the industrial force for the first time in large numbers. With their new economic clout, members of these groups demanded equal political status; in time the law gave formal recognition to this status. Racial segregation and the status of wives as chattel were not abolished because of some massive change of heart by the government but because of changing social realities.

(b) Technological Change—According to McLuhan, changes in technology bring with them changes in sensory modalities and sensibilities. That is, with new technologies, new ways of perceiving the world and relating to others follow. Thus in electrical societies the relationships amongst people is different from those in mechanical societies and both are different from those in primitive agrarian societies. As a result, the laws appropriate for electrical societies differ from those in agrarian societies. In the cases referred to, it is clear that the laws regulating marital relationships in the largely rural, early industrial society of the Atwoods were different from those of the more highly developed industrial society of the Jackson and both had to differ from the rules of the advanced-industrial or postindustrial society of Becker and Pettkus. Modern societies require more innovative, resourceful literate people, not passive, conforming citizens. Restrictions and privileges on the basis of sex are irrelevant, if not counterproductive in our contemporary competitive societies.

(c) Changing Values and Perceptions—With social, economic and technological changes the feudal society with its belief in natural, hierarchical order gave way to the ideals of efficient production in pragmatic and utilitarian outlooks. Certainly efficiency was a primary value of industrial societies. Thus the focus gradually shifted from sex and social position to skills and abilities. As a result, the importance of being male was reduced, and ceased being the only basis of power and authority in the family. Universal rights slowly began to replace privilege by sex. As a result equal opportunity became the cornerstone of the emerging industrial democracy, though not actual equality. No legal system has gone this far.

(d) Laws and Legal Principles—Though attention must be paid to the material conditions of society, one cannot understand legal change without reference to the laws operating in society and the principles underlying court judgments. This should be amply clear from the case study in this chapter which showed the slow movement from principles and laws based on a paternalistic form of natural law to those based on humanistic concepts.

The foregoing are some of the sorts of factors that account for legal change. As Mr. Justice Dickson states, more than legal principles enter into legal judgments. However legal judgments do enter and should not be reduced to other factors.

•In effect a very complex notion of law emerges. Law as process is historical in nature. It develops over time and incorporates rational responses *and* social, economic and political forces. because law is a conscious, rational response guiding social action, history cannot be understood without law. Conversely because law is a social process, law cannot be understood without history.

•Legal developments can only be understood after they have occurred. In 1718 the process culminating the *Pettkus v Becker* was unknowable. Moreover the significance of the Agar-Ellis, Jackson and Persons cases could not be fully appreciated. Their full meaning could only be understood long after they occurred. It is possible that decisions in the future will render the pattern of change and its significance radically different. For what the pattern is, depends on what the future will be. In a significant way, the future determines what the past was. Thus the pattern the process of law takes is subject to change, hence is open.

•The implications of education of this view are considerable. To understand law one must not only understand the nature of rules, principles, the modes of judgment and the institution of law. One must understand law as an historical process, the values and calculations of the parties involved in the dispute, the social forces, the technological superstructure, economic conditions, social values and many other factors combining to form a very pervasive dynamic process. Unfortunately, few educators of law appreciate the complexity of the law in sufficient measure and most at the secondary and professional levels deal with law as if it were a self-subsisting entity. To expect better may be asking too much.

But how good can better be? This is the topic of the following chapter.

Notes

1. Edward H. Levi, *An Introduction to Legal Reasoning* (Chicago: University of Chicago Press, 1948, 1970), 1.
2. *Ibid.*, 4.
3. *Ibid.*, 1-2.
4. *Ibid.*, 8-9.
5. 5 Maule and Selwyn 198 (1816).
6. 199, quoted in Levi, 10.
7. 6 N.Y. 397 (1852).
8. 217 N.Y. 382, 111 N. E. 1050 (1916).
9. 217 N.Y. 382, 396, 111 N.E. 1050, 1055 (1916), quoted in Levi, 21.
10. *Atwood v. Atwood* (1718) Prec Ch. 492; Gilb Ch. 149; 24 E.R. 220.
11. *I Corinthians* 11:3 and 11:7; *Ephesians* 5:22 and 23.
12. Sir William Blackstone, *Commentaries of the Laws of England*, 1770. Selections appear in G. Jones, ed., *The Sovereignty of Law* (University of Toronto Press, 1973).
13. *Rex v. Manneville* (1804) 5 East 221.
14. *Rex v. Greenhill* (1836) 4 Ad. and El. 624.
15. *Re Cochrane* (1840) 8 Dowl 630; 4 Jar 535.
16. *Ex Parte Sandilands* (1852) 21 LJQB, 342.
17. 343.
18. See G. M. Young, *Victorian England, Portrait of an Age* for a superb account of some of these conflicts.

19. See *Besant v. Wood* (1878). Proc Chancery Court, 1878.
20. *In re Agar-Ellis* (1878), 24 GR.D. 317.
21. *The Queen v. Jackson* (1891), I.Q.B. 671
22. *Ibid.*, 679.
23. *Ibid.*, 681.
24. *Ibid.*, 682.
25. *Ibid.*, 681.
26. *Ibid.*, 679.
27. Dominion Law Reports, 1930, 99.
28. *Murdoch v. Murdoch* (1973) 41 D.L.R. (3d), 373.
29. *Ibid.*, 388.
30. *Rathwell v. Rathwell* (1978) 2 S.C.R. 436?
31. *Pettkus v. Becker* (1980) 2 S.C.R., 834.
32. *Ibid.*, 850.
33. *Ibid.*, 844, see also 2 *SCR*, 455.
34. *See Brooks et al. v. U.I.C.*, D.L.R., 1989.
35. Quoted in *The Toronto Star*, 5 May 1989, A5.
36. *Loc Cit.*
37. *Loc Cit.*
38. *The Charter of Rights and Freedoms: A Guide for Canadians* (Ottawa: Publications Canada, 1984, 15.
39. *Ibid.*, 16.
40. *Ibid.*, 29.
41. *Ibid.*, 30.
42. *Rathwell v. Rathwell* (1978), 2 S.C.R., 436.

6

Law in Itself

Reflections on Law as Process

The view developed on the previous chapter, that law can be seen as a continuous and connected historical process in which specific legal judgments are made in response to existing conditions and previous conceptions, appears at first sight to be a plausible one, even a satisfying one. It is a view based on verifiable evidence. It accounts for change in law and changes in laws. It enables us to see the overriding patterns in existence at any time. And it explains how the law got to where it is. In effect the flux of social existence, and the rules and principles governing it can be grasped and inspected to the degree that they allow. Only the frozen and the static can be seen in terms of absoluteness and permanence. Any clear observation of the law reveals it to be neither, so it seemed.

Still, at some level, this view is not, I believe, entirely satisfying. Somehow it does not get to the most essential elements of law. As a result it does not do the job we want a theory to do.

Law as Historical Process is law observed. Though it is law observed over a long historical period and not law observed in its operation at a specific time and place, as Law as Rules is, it remains an external conception (or perspective) of an essentially internal phenomenon. It is present thought *about* law and as such freezes law. It is not law as it unfolds itself or in itself. As such, the law referred to is static or grasped law, not dynamic law in a true sense. The common belief that studies of processes somehow reveal the essence(s) of dynamic phenomena is false since the studies themselves impose extrinsic categories on the phenomena and fail to take their own involvement in the study into account. Unless conceptions or views of law somehow get to law as such, then they miss something critical and are mere fabrications of our imagination.

But, is it even possible to get to this ultimate level? Can we know law as it really is? Can we know anything about such law? Can we ever know there really is such a thing as law? Quite possibly, the answer to all these questions is "no." Certainly, we cannot know much of substance about law as such. However it is important to determine how much or how little we can know and what sort of things we can know about law in itself, if we are to understand the nature of law. Thus this chapter.

The Elusive, Inaccessible Dimension of Law

At this point a very brief summary may help to avoid unnecessary confusion. Throughout this work it has been maintained, and at times argued, that there is a fundamental indeterminacy involved in using any rational method for understanding and controlling society in general and law in particular. Because rational method cannot take rational method into account in the study of society/law then the nature of society/law is indeterminate. By classifying, correlating, predicting, and explaining, we engage in procedures that affect what we purport to know yet do not and cannot take into account how the procedures themselves affect outcomes not how such procedures come about. Further, it is held that such procedures fail to reach in any significant way, the essential aspects of nonsubjective reality, the thing itself "out there." Something crucial, self-subsistent and independent is missed. However, this latter claim is by no means universally accepted. On the contrary it is nearly universally rejected as unknowable and as having no grounds for belief. To a great extent I share this view, but those considerations creating occasional doubts in my mind about it may be of great philosophical and social importance especially as it pertains to law.

Critical questions arise. Are there some universal features shared by all legal systems suggesting an independent core of law itself? Are there some laws or substantive matters that law *must* have? Obviously not. As shown in the previous chapter, the substance of law changes over time as social conditions and values change. Even where all societies have prohibitions against theft, the meaning or nature of theft varies. For example, the theft of television signals in electronic societies differs from the theft of sheep in a feudal society and the theft of a birthright in ancient nomadic societies. In fact, such a concept of theft would be incomprehensible in preelectronic societies. So there are no absolute, universal, necessary laws. Is there then not some universal *process* of law or at least features that must be shared by all systems? Lon Fuller, in *The*

Morality of the Law, argues that there are at least eight ways *not* to make a law, including having conflicting laws, not publicizing laws, governing authorities not abiding by their own rules, generating laws on an ad hoc basis, and so on. According to Fuller, this suggests universal structural principles. But even it if did, these are not distinctively legal principles but principles of good management for any institution. Besides ad hocery, retroactivity and inconsistency abound in most legal systems if not in all, thus Fuller's structural principles are by no means necessary. Thus there is no specific substance nor structures universally shared by law.

A more basic question is whether there is some final authority in law that is decisive and in which all procedures come to rest. In other words, does law necessitate a process in which some stable manner of judgment exists? Once again a negative answer must be given to these questions. For there is no ultimate source or procedure in making legal judgments that would be an essential part of Law in Itself. An illustration of this can be found in the recent reversal by the Chief Justice of the Supreme Court of Canada. Mr. Justice Dickson, in 1977, denied a woman's claim to receive unemployment insurance benefits for the period she had taken off work to give birth. After all, it was reasoned, it is a fact of nature that a woman can give birth to children, and this fact cannot be ignored in determining her rights. In effect, the exercise of a woman's natural capacity to bear children can be taken as legitimate grounds for the denial of insurance benefits for the period taken. One's rights are not independent of one's nature. However, in 1989, Dickson declared that one could *not* justify the loss of such benefits by a woman because she had given birth, because the loss would be discriminatory against women. If so, the facts of nature have no bearing on morality, specifically on social values. Such matters, he reasoned, are legal matters. What is significant in these cases, aside from the explicit rejection of Natural Law by the Supreme Court, is the indeterminacy of the process. Though lower court decisions can be overturned by higher courts, the Supreme Court is supposedly the ultimate judge or final arbiter. But it is not, in the sense that it can later reverse itself as the foregoing case and probably the Murdoch case show. Thus not only are substantive matters related to unemployment benefits or property rights in marriage *essentially* arbitrary, or at least relative to rapidly changing conceptions and values, so are procedural matters as when retroactive legislation pertaining to war crimes is considered valid legislation, when it had previously been considered invalid, or when individuals are tried for crimes committed in a place where the court has previously not had jurisdiction.

If, then, there is no determinate substance of law and no discrete process or procedures, nor any *final* authority, what is law? Is it a purely human invention, reinvented in every society and meaningful only for that society? What connection would there be between different systems of law? Would the various concepts of law have no connection with one another, hence mean totally different things in different systems? Or is there something that exists, in some sense, that all refer to? If there is, what can be said about it, in what ways can it affect us—either because it is known or because it is unknowable?

The most notable attempt to answer similar fruitless questions was made by Kant. As am I today, so was Kant over two centuries, ago driven to ask these questions. At the very outset of his *Critique of Pure Reason* he remarks,

> Human reason has this peculiar fate that in one species of its knowledge it is burdened by questions which, as prescribed by the very nature of reason itself, it is not able to ignore, but which, as transcending all its powers, it is also not able to answer.[1]

That such questions pose themselves seems evident. Whether *no* answers to them are possible is not as evident.

Kant himself distinguished between two realms, the phenomenal, or the realm of appearances, and the noumenal, or the realm of things in themselves. In modern jargon, the former would be the constructions of reality created by humans, the latter reality as it is in itself. While professing to believe that human understanding is limited to the phenomenal realm, which is constructed in space and time with the universally shared categories of quantity, quality, relationship, and modality, he could not avoid discussing things in themselves, especially in the realms of morality and aesthetic judgment. Strictly speaking, it is an error to apply the categories of understanding to things in themselves, and by saying things in themselves exist and have some effect on our perception, Kant violated his own rules.

However in discussing the noumenon, Kant asserts that we can say nothing substantive about it. There can be no science of things in themselves. The most we can do is see it as a limit to our understanding, a border understanding cannot cross.

Even though the Kantian distinctions are far from clear and the concept of noumenon itself problematic, his notion of thing in itself may be helpful for a fuller understanding of law. If indeed there is some basic core of law, something describable as Law in Itself, it may at best be knowable only as a limit. As such, nothing specific can be stated about that which it encompasses as a limit. One cannot properly say what law is, for this would require going beyond what one is entitled to. One can only say there is something, and it imposes limits because its specific features are beyond our grasp. The implications of all this is that there is a law and it is real. As such we are making a substantive claim of sorts. We know there is something beyond the limits, but what that is cannot be know in detail.

However, such a belief should not arise without grounds or reasons or some consciously compelling force. If it did, it would be no more than just another dogma. There must, in effect, be some basis for believing in the existence of so strange a thing. But one believes in the existence of things for many different reasons, sometimes on intuitive grounds where some basic things are known directly and immediately. Other times we believe in the existence of things because it "makes sense" to do so and it does not "make sense" not to do so.

The view that the way we function in the world (i.e., how we do things) somehow constitutes the nature of this world is a fairly common theme in twentieth-century thought. As noted, Heisenberg claimed that one's means of measurement constituted the natural object measured in science, and this led to a basic indeterminacy in nature. On such a view, the notion of an independent nature with features of its own becomes a fiction. The Kantian noumenon or thing in itself is finally laid to rest. It can tell us nothing and is of no use.

A similar rejection or perhaps avoidance of the noumenon is implicit in the theories of Marshall McLuhan. In McLuhan's system, the technology used in any society affects the sensibilities of its users and determines what they know. How one does things determines what one knows. There is no independent reality out there to be grasped by the neutral, independent thought and reason of human beings. Rather, the "medium is the message."[2] Hence, those living in societies using electronic technology perceive, feel, think and function differently from those living in societies using mechanical tools and those living in preindustrial feudal societies. Similarly literate people are fundamentally different in all respects from preliterate people. Basically, all humans are affected by their environment, an environment resulting not only from the physical qualities of society but more from the nature of the technology of production and communication. According to McLuhan, one's environment is really a condition of perception, knowing, and so on and not something that is itself perceived. All social environments are themselves invisible, and not something the social inhabitants are aware of. Thus McLuhan makes the insightful claim noted in the first chapter of this work, "we don't know who discovered water, but we are sure it wasn't a fish."[3] And, as with Heisenberg, McLuhan seems to reject the notion of noumenon, or at the very least is silent about it.

However, such a view, is not without its serious problems. If indeed all conceptions are dependent on and to some extent determined by the technology prevailing in their environment, then McLuhan's own concepts cannot be exempt. If so, then his views are simply environment-bound perceptions/conceptions of a person living in contemporary North American society. In no way can these views be said to represent the knowledge and experience of Homeric Greeks, Ming dynasty Chinese, Renaissance Italians, or even present-day Russians. Their conceptions are not McLuhan's conceptions. These conceptions arose out of different environments, with different technologies so that even the terms "environment" and "technology" are not comparable. Yet McLuhan blithely persists in informing his readers/listeners how Greeks, Chinese, and Russians live in different worlds from us, experience things differently and conceive things differently. At one level, he rejects any common reality, yet at another level he assumes that he has insight into Reality, with a capital "R." Unfortunately, he never explicitly recognizes the latter. Such a recognition, I suspect, involves a belief in an independent existence.

How one is to reveal the existence of the noumenon or Reality in Itself is a critical matter for all noumenalists, even "noumenalist minimalists" like myself. The most obvious way is to show that some such assumption is somehow implicit in all theories of nature and society, even theories of those who deny it, as McLuhan and Heisenberg appear to. A related way is to show that the assumption of a noumenon is a condition for possible knowledge of nature and society. This task is much more difficult, if not impossible, because the very use of structures, of tools, of institutions, of measuring devices, even of concepts preclude the accessibility to an independent noumenon. If one finds genuine contradictions in theories unacceptable as I do, then one seems to be at a theoretical impasse. However, not everyone is intimidated by contradictions and such a person gets around the impasse by confounding us with pronouncements about the nature of dialectics and esoteric theories of dialectics, as if labelling a process "dialectical" allows contradiction and implausibility to be feasible.

Spengler: The Independent Reality Underlying History

Perhaps one way of getting a handle on the concept of noumenal law is through a consideration of some of the historical-philosophical views of Oswald Spengler in his monumental work *The Decline of the West*. In spite of some questionable metaphors and absurd claims, Spengler presents a number of original and suggestive ideas on the development of social forms and practices. According to Spengler (reflecting on nine thousand years of human history), there is an unfolding of an inescapable, natural process in history, in which cultures arise and fall in one thousand year cycles, independently of the attempts of individuals or peoples to shape their own destinies. Each culture goes through four seasons—Spring, Summer, Autumn, and Winter.

In Spring, a culture goes through a crude, primitive but highly energetic phase. Spengler describes the phase as "rural-intuitive," indicating both its locale and *modus operandi*. At this time "great creations of the newly awakened dream-heavy Soul"[4] are produced. It is the time that great myths and folk tales are spawned. Far from being dry, lethargic, or intellectual in nature, it is a time of enormous energy, spontaneity, unreflective, and remorseless cruelty.

In Summer, consciousness first ripens. It too is a time of great activity with conquests and exploration taking place. Characteristically, great risks are taken spontaneously at great costs to all involved. It is a time of renaissance, of the founding of social groupings and of the invention of basic geometry and arithmetic. It is a time when individuals begin to become differentiated within the group that continues to display its great energy.

By Autumn, the Creative Intellect has taken over. It is a time when great art, philosophy, music, and architecture are produced. In keeping with these developments, society becomes urbanized, though it remains largely rural. In this period of an emergent rationalism and enlightenment, cultures become intellectually alive but lose their raw, explosive physical energy.

Finally, in Winter, Culture becomes Civilization. Spontaneity declines. Energy wanes. The rural base becomes urban and the center of civilization is the megalopolis, the massive city. Intuition is systematically replaced by rational, formal thinking. Everything in life is seen as a problem to be solved by rational formula. Decline has set in and the end of the Civilization is approaching. All rational attempts to stem the flow are futile. Thus rational method, far from being a source of power and means of control, is really a sign of historical decline. In effect rationality and decline are historically and necessarily connected.

In essence, Spengler has claimed that quite apart from conscious human endeavor, some "hidden" process of history is occurring. In this process, a determinate pattern unfolds. *It* happens. We do not make it happen—though we often deceive ourselves in believing that our consciousness, planning, analysis, and reasoning enable us to overcome the problems confronting humanity. Spengler views rationality, not as the master of history but as one of its effects. Rationality, itself is taken as an object and fits into a pattern that is observed. Once this is done, the human element in the construction of Reality is transformed from active determinant to passive determined. Something is happening to us quite independently of our deliberations and actions.

Of course Spengler confuses the issue by claiming to describe and explain the process. If he were consistent, which he is not, he would admit that this great force is cognitively unknowable. He would somehow become aware of his own intellectualism, an intellectualism that identifies with its enemy, and conclude that it is distortive and impotent. Instead he concludes that Reality is knowable, but uncontrollable. He cannot escape his rationalism.

But even if one were to take Spengler with a grain of salt, even recognizing the validity of Thomas Mann's assessment of Spengler as a fascist and as "the hyena of history," one may find in his howlings some insightful suggestions into the workings of society today. For one thing, the obsessively legalistic society we live in seems to reflect a cautious, controlled rationalism in which there is a fear to trust one's intuitions and immediate responses, and to act or do things spontaneously. More and more there is the tendency to think things through, to plan every conceivable course of action. With our obsession with rules, policies, principles, objectives, strategies, rights, details, and so on, social existence is increasingly being programmed and social relationships subjected to predefined legal rules and principles. Ours is a society obsessed with forms and formal principles even in the area of fundamental moral decisions and choices, as the theories of such influential psychologists as Piaget and Kohlberg reflect. Ours is a society of growing bureaucracies, created to administer the formalization of humanity. It is also a society of judicial burnout at the highest level amidst vain attempts to get control of the mass of problems. It is a society that could grind to a halt without knowing it.

One of Spengler's notable insights is that there is a world independent of human thought affecting human cultures. He perceived from his reading of history that rationality did not guarantee control. As a formalized, general method of perceiving and planning, rationality became an object, hence could be categorized, analyzed, and studied. As such rationality became part of the observed process not its external shaper and manipulator. Thus implicit in Spengler's system is a union of noumenon and phenomenon, of a self-subsistent process and of worlds conceived at different times and places by different modes of perception. Of course Spengler says more than he should about this independent process. His metaphors relating the emergence of cultures to seasons and historical processes to flowers blooming and withering amount to a system that serves as much as a straitjacket on an independent process as does rationality. But such absurdities should not detract from his insights.

In contrast, Kant consistently attempted to separate the Reality (noumenon) from the social constructions (phenomenon). How we know self-subsistent Reality is different from how we know the world of nature. The two worlds could never really come together in one system, on such a view. But in spite of his Herculean philosophical attempts, the shadow of the noumenon never left the phenomenon and the two remained inextricably connected. In the Spenglerian system, the two come together with the noumenon as Reality prevailing. Intuitive spontaneous humans are closest to being agents. Rational beings are not doers, but are done to. Spengler's conception of the relationship between rationality and freedom is markedly different from Kant's conception that rationality entails freedom and that rational moral agents are autonomous. What is mysterious in Kant's writings is how autonomous beings, authentic doers, can perform in a phenomenal world, a world constituted by constructs, by the categories of the understanding not of their making.

The fullest and most striking expression of the view that social and natural reality as we know them are constructs of the human mind is made in the writings of Ludwig Wittgenstein. Prior to Kant, philosophers attempted to get to Reality from the perceptions or sensations of human beings. After Kant, the focus was placed increasingly on the categories the mind provided. And most recently the focus has been on the nature of language and symbols. These views generally restrict knowable reality to whatever is constituted by words, concepts, symbols, and the like.

Excursions beyond this realm smell of metaphysics and are avoided, even if self-subsistent realities are not explicitly denied.

Wittgenstein writes:

> To give the essence of proposition means to give the essence of all description, therefore the essence of the world.[5]

He clarifies this somewhat in another passage:

> That the world is *my* world shows itself in the fact that the limits of my language (of the only language I can understand) mean the limits of my world.[6]

It is, thus, only if one has language that one has a world in which he/she exists. Such language provides the limits of *my* world. There is no such thing as "the world" mentioned except as reduced to *my* world. Wittgenstein develops this position even further in a later work. He writes,

> clearly the words "Now I am seeing this as the apex" cannot so far mean anything to a learner who has only just met the concepts of apex, base, and so on. — But I do not mean this as an empirical proposition.
>
> "Now he is seeing it like *this*", "now like *that*" would only be said of someone *capable* of making certain applications of the figure quite freely.[7]

On this view one cannot be said to see something (or feel or smell it) unless one had the concepts necessarily associated with that thing and could correctly apply these concepts. Thus one can be said to see the apex of a triangle only if one had the concept of apex and related concepts and knew when and how to apply them. An implication of such a view is that the very existence of a world for anyone is that one have a language and know how to apply its concepts.

This view is supported by Peter Winch in his commentary on the foregoing passages. Winch writes that

> in discussing language philosophically we are in fact discussing *what counts as belonging to the world*. Our idea of what belongs to the realm of reality is given for us in the language that we use there is no way of getting outside the concepts in terms of which we think of this world. The world *is* for us what is presented through these concepts. That is not to say that our concepts may not change; but when they do, that means that our concept of the world has changed too.[8]

Once again the view is expressed that the only reality we know and experience is the phenomenal reality. Just as we cannot get outside of our bodies to do something, we cannot get outside the concepts of our language to understand *our* world. Whether there is a reality beyond such concepts or whether there is a reality underlying such concepts, cannot be addressed philosophically. To apprehend such reality would require going beyond possible language. To know what this would be, would itself require the use of concepts, hence is self-defeating. On such philosophical tangles, Wittgenstein has his admonitions. Thus in the last line of the Tractatus he writes,

> What we cannot speak about we must pass over in silence.[9]

Wittgenstein, to my understanding (or reading), did remain silent on fundamentals, as did McLuhan. Kant tried to be silent on substantive matters, though not on formal principles, and had problems. Spengler showed no inclination to silence and as a result said nonsensical things, but he did grapple with an important specter, Reality.

As already noted, such a specter must somehow be understood, if law is to be understood at a more than superficial level. Ours is an age of rationalization of society, to a great extent. Governments grow, bureaucracies cannot be contained, and law expands within existing realms and into new realms. The appetites of rationalizers seem insatiable. Yet to say that these outcomes are rationally planned is clearly false. If so, we must come to some understanding of the larger process that law and other social institutions are somehow subjected to, a process that goes beyond providing specific legal solutions to specific social problems.

What Can We Know About Law in Itself?

In contrast to the reasonable caution of Kant, Wittgenstein and McLuhan, though not contrary to some of their implicit assumptions, I will try to suggest the plausibility of a number of (claims) assertions.

1.   First, I will try to support the belief that there is such a thing as Law in Itself or Noumenal law. This involves indicating *that* there is such a thing as Law in Itself, *why* I believe in such a thing, *what* it is, and *how* it operates, to the limited extent that these are possible.

Such an argument, if it is an argument, will draw on some of Spengler's insights and apply them to contemporary law.

2.   I will then try to show that there is a connection between there being Law in Itself and a form of social indeterminacy. What this means and why it occurs are critical and my views on these matters will be based on some of John Austin's views of language that go beyond the abstract generalities of Wittgenstein's philosophical statements quoted earlier.

3.   In doing so, I will provide a partial explanation of why the legal system is the prime contributor to both social anarchy and social order. This discussion will draw on the claims made in the other two sections, hence will draw on my view of how law operates today as well as on Austin's theories of language.

It was earlier noted that Spengler's views about the rationalism characterizing twentieth century Western society (even seventy years after *The Decline of West*) are plausible and that the connection between rationalism and decline is not totally off the wall. The evidence supporting the view that we live in a legalistic society characterized by an obsessive rationalism is overwhelming. Every social activity is measured, correlated, and predicted; moral behavior is reduced to reasoning, ordered in sequential, law-governed stages; mind is seen as a computing machine with programs governed by mechanical laws. Everything we do is subsumed under a formula or clearly articulated principle. The primary justification for this—as if we had control of the process —is that by knowing what to expect, we will be in a position to control the outcomes of "the system"—as if we live in a system.

The possible irony in all this is that it is more than conceivable that in spite of better, clearer, more equitable laws, society is becoming less manageable. While more and more laws are created, more and more deals are made out of court to keep the legal system from grinding to a halt because of work overload and jurist burnout.[10] So in spite of a great legal system in theory, society may be going all to hell on roller skates.

Perhaps this is not too surprising. Just as a highly developed science is often a response to, or even a function of, military and political needs, as well as grim social problems (e.g., the AIDS epidemic), so a highly refined legal system may be a response to or a function of a growing pathology in society. And just as a great science may indicate serious problems of one sort, so a highly developed legal system may indicate an underlying chaos or social disorder. In neither case do advancements necessarily stop the process. They are part of it. For there appears to be a much more fundamental process unfolding, a process that encompasses rational decision making and at some basic level is unaffected by it. If so, law may have an inner dynamic of its own quite apart from the rational formulations of judges and politicians and distinct from the patterns determined in legal and historical inquiries.

Though there are essential differences between the two, it may be helpful to draw an analogy between the inner dynamic of law and the inner workings of institutions, as depicted in chapter 2. It was noted that in spite of conscious attempts to control and use institutions as means of achieving determinate social goals, institutions invariably develop structures of their own and develop in ways quite distinct from the rational calculations of the designers of the institutions and the programs. Institutions (especially total institutions) always develop control mechanisms that are not needed nor even useful in achieving officially proclaimed goals. Thus psychiatric hospitals provide services that may help cure mental illness for some patients in accordance with the proclaimed goals of these hospitals, or schools provide programs which may help educate some students, but both institutions develop manipulative structures quite apart from, and often detrimental to therapy and education. In both cases, as with other institutions, the survival of the institution as such, apart from achieving its proclaimed goals, becomes an important consideration and internal procedures and mechanisms of control develop accordingly, whether or not their administrations and staff are conscious of it.[11] In effect, the emergence of control cannot be controlled.

The institution of law seems to develop in a similar way. As do other institutions, law tends to grow and grow, constantly appropriating more powers to itself until it becomes forbidding on the outside and unmanageable from the inside. Paradoxically, any attempt (short of revolution) to curtail the power of law would itself require law. Thus in order to stop growing, it frequently has to grow. Yet in spite of the growth and increased power of law, it may not be any more effective that it was and may even be losing control. The unfolding of the legal process seems to be part of a broader phenomenon captured so strikingly in the opening sentence of Saul Pett's Pulitzer Prize-winning portrait of the U.S. government: "The government of the United States is so big that nobody runs it and nobody owns it."[12] Nobody has to run government.

It runs itself. So does law. That is why politicians and lawyers never have to worry that the state will wither away, under capitalism, socialism, or even anarchism. They will never be lacking for "work."

However law is unlike other institutions in several crucial respects. It is more basic than others in that *it* creates the formal conditions that make other institutions possible—with the possible exception of the State, which seems coextensive with the law. Yet in creating these conditions, the law seems to generate circumstances beyond the realm of human control. It seems to go its own ineffable way.

Law is also distinctive in that language functions within it in a distinctive way. As in all social discourse, language constitutes the world referred to and lived in. Certainly, in some respects Wittgenstein's claim that the limits of my language are the limits of my world is plausible. So is his claim that to perceive the apex of a triangle one must have the concepts of apex, base, triangle, and must know how to apply them correctly. It would follow from these assertions that to function in society or within a legal system one must have determinate social and legal concepts that constitute the social and legal realms and one must know how to apply them.

To a significant extent Wittgenstein's analysis provides great insights into the relationship between language and reality. However, I have two reservations about his views. First, it does not explicitly allow for the existence and influence of the noumenal realm upon individuals in a law-regulated society. Things happen to us that are beyond our control whether we have concepts of these things or not. Society goes its own way and carries us with it, whether or not we conceptualize it in minute detail. To try to understand such happenings one need not try to employ concepts in the precise rule-governed way we do in more accessible social situations. Suggestions, hints, metaphors, and other indirect methods may be necessary. Good intuitions may be more useful than formidable reasoning powers. Secondly, the level of explanation of personal and social reality in the passages quoted is too abstract and general. While it may be useful to know that a language or conceptual system is necessary for providing "a description" of a social or legal realm, or any other realm for that matter, it does not tell us enough, certainly not everything that is crucial. For language does much more than describe. What is needed is a specific theory of *how* language affects legal reality and *what* the connection between language and Law in Itself is. Such a theory will not only enable us to understand descriptions "of our own legal reality," it should also enable us to understand how our legal system *itself* works, its inner dynamic. In my view, the writings of John Austin on language provide some of the important insights into such a theory.

However, in order to connect Austin's conceptions of language to Law in Itself and indeterminacy in law it is necessary to look more closely and specifically at Law in Itself. First the question of whether there is any evidence or grounds for holding the view that there is an independent process of law must be considered. While there may be considerable evidence to support specific views about trends in law, such as the growth of law as an instrument of social, control or the increase in political and economic rights by women in North American Society, there may be problems in establishing conclusively that law has a dynamic of its own beyond human control or that law creates circumstances that are at times unforeseeable. For something more than empirical evidence is needed to suggest that independent unforeseeable processes occur. At heart, there is a structural and conceptual element involved. For the belief in interdeterminacy rests on the way one views and ought to view the world, the way one sees language and the connections between the two. Merely because no one has ever determined X, it does not follow that X is indeterminable. In effect it requires going to a deeper level of analysis of legal phenomena, a level beyond the straight empirical.

The Indeterminacy of Legislation: Case Studies

In recent legal history, it would appear that there are several phenomena that have taken place that lend themselves most easily to the conception of law that I am advocating. One example of legislation creating a new political, social and economic dynamic that was unforeseen and almost certainly unforeseeable is the Eighteenth Amendment of the U.S. Constitution of 1920, known generally as the Prohibition Act, but more formally as the Volstead Act. With great clarity and directness, this legislation not only banned the manufacture, sale, and transportation of *all* intoxicating beverages, it entrenched this prohibition within the U.S. Constitution.[13]

Attempts to bring about total prohibition originated in the nineteenth century, if not earlier, in the U.S. and were supported by such notables as Lyman Beecher and the millions belonging to the so-called temperance societies.[14] Although temperance supporters have received a bad press in the past half century, their program was based on solid, rational grounds. In part, at least, the Volstead Act was created as a rational response to the devastation of American society caused by alcoholic drink. The evangelist preacher Billy Sunday, one of the most forceful and influential advocates of prohibition, noted in his sermons how rural America had degenerated because of alcohol.[15] Poor farmers would drive to town in their horses and wagons, with their wives and children, to buy provisions for the week. Before beginning their shopping, they would go into the saloon "for one drink," while their families waited on the wagon. Several hours later, they would emerge—drunk, broke, guilty, and angry. The result was the starvation of the family and the physical abuse of their wives and children. Sunday also supported his prohibitionist position by citing the enormous cost alcohol carried with its use. The cost of health care facilities, psychiatric treatment, crime and corruption due to the drinking of alcohol were too great to bear—in the hundreds of millions of dollars annually. At another level the Volstead Act was an attempt by rural, Protestant America to resist the tide of the urban, polyglot culture that was swamping America. Billy Sunday and his supporters dreamt of a return to the simple rural life, based on the patriarchal family, sobriety, the Protestant work ethic, and a Biblical morality. For Billy Sunday, "The saloon is the crime of cities."[16] and "[farmers] are the best class of men on God's dirt."[17] Thus he reasoned that the outlawing of spirits would result in a tranquil, harmonious society, based on religion (i.e., Protestant fundamentalism), the family and old-fashioned morality.

But, instead, this legislation unleashed new forces in American society that no one anticipated and few wished for. As Richard Hofstadter wrote in the preface to Andrew Sinclair's *Prohibition: The Era of Excess,*

> the imposition of controls led to a loss of control; the churches created gangsters; reformers became reactionaries; purifiers became poisoners.[18]

Somehow the magnitude of the catastrophe created by what seemed to many clear-thinking citizens to be a rational response to a crippling social and moral problem was unforeseeable. To those responsible for dealing with the fallout, the problem was overwhelming.

> Fiorello La Guardia who became mayor of New York in 1934, calculated that Gotham's tipplers supported twenty-two thousand speakeasies. He startled even hardbitten New Yorkers with his estimate that to enforce the Volstead Act properly would require 250,000 cops—plus a further 200,000 super-policemen to keep the first group within the law. Worst of all between 1920 and 1930 some

thirty-four thousand Americans died from alcohol poisoning; two thousand gangsters and five hundred prohibition agents were killed in the many gunfights triggered by the trade's excesses.[19]

Suddenly new names were evoked as the prime movers in American Society. Presidents such as Coolidge and Hoover were not seen as the leaders and shapers of society. Instead, Capone, Remus, McCoy (the real McCoy!), Moran, Rosenstiel, Torrio, Dutch Schultz, Licavoli, and the like were referred to with awe and fascination. Great fortunes were made, some lost, others built on. And society was transformed as perhaps never before.

Without prohibition, Al Capone would have remained a small-time hoodlum. Because of the huge stakes involved, crime became better organized and more brutal and emerged as a major force in politics as well as the economy. This is indicated by the much quoted but never challenged remark of Meyer Lansky, the financial brains of the so-called Mafia: "We're bigger than U.S. Steel." Without prohibition, conditions would not have allowed new major political forces as the Kennedys to play so major a role in American politics. For with the failure of prohibition the dominance of rural, Protestant and Anglo-Saxon power groups receded, making possible a Roman Catholic president a quarter of a century later. Moreover, without prohibition the multinational conglomerate Seagram's Corporation, one of the largest corporations in North America, and perhaps the world, would not exist. This has been explicitly asserted because of "the undeniable fact that the Bronfman fortune was squarely based on supplying American bootleggers with their wares."[20] And without prohibition, the emergence of individuals of Irish, Jewish, Italian, German and other ethnic backgrounds in the American establishment would not have occurred as it did, nor would the impact of shifts in power in politics and the economy have been the same. Nor would the corruption of politicians and police officials have occurred and persisted as it did.

In all this some perplexing questions must be asked. Why is it that an apparently rational solution to a most grievous and debilitating socioeconomic problem was a key factor in generating the destructive chaos of the Prohibition Era? Why were the consequences of this legislation not foreseen in its full seriousness? Why, in fact, were these consequences unforeseeable?

To begin to answer these and related questions, one must gain some understanding of the language of law. One must go beyond the generalities of Wittgenstein's vague assertions that the limits of my language are the limits of my world. One must go the way language functions.

Language and Social Reality

According to John Austin,[21] linguistic statements can function in two distinct ways. Some statements serve to describe, report or inform about a state of affairs. Each statement of this type must be either true or false. Such statements are called "Informative statements." Examples of informative statements are:

"It is now raining in Toronto"

"Washington is the capitol of Canada."

"Caesar crossed the Rubicon in 44 B.C."

"Cats have 10 legs."

In contrast, other sorts of statements (or utterances), in their very statement or utterance *do* something, perform an action. *As such*, they do not report anything, hence cannot be either true or false. Such statements are called "Performative Statements" or more commonly "Performative Utterances." Examples of such statements are:

"I promise to repay this loan by Saturday."

"I name this ship the Queen Elizabeth."

"I hereby bequeath this watch to my brother."

"I now pronounce you man and wife."

"Charge!" (Order given by officer in battle.)

Each of these statements does something. The first statement *makes* a promise; it creates something that did not exist prior to its utterance. The second formally names a ship, the third utterance actually assigns ownership of a watch upon the death of the bequeather. And so on. In all cases something is added to an existing reality and the statement is uttered precisely to do this. The function of such statements is not to describe anything truly, hence cannot be true or false.

It should be noted, however, that the mere pronouncement of the words does not create the action. For successful performances to occur, specific conditions must be fulfilled. Thus a clergyman uttering "I now pronounce you man and wife" to a consenting couple who have correctly completed all the necessary forms, have had the necessary blood tests, are of an age of majority, and so on has successfully married the couple. However the local barber saying the same thing to two five year olds has not.

For an utterance or set of utterances to be a proper performative utterance, at least six conditions must be met, according to Austin. First, there must be some accepted conventional procedure. The procedure must take place under appropriate circumstances with appropriate people. Procedures must be executed correctly. They must also be executed completely. The speaker must be sincere in his/her pronouncements. Thus one does not execute a promise if one has no intention of keeping it, regardless of what one says. And finally the participants in the action must subsequently behave in a manner that is appropriate for that action. If any of these conditions is violated then the performance would likely be seen as "infelicitous," but never as "false"—except in a metaphorical sense.

However, Austin was keenly aware of the difficulties in coming up with a neat theory of performative utterances. He recognized that there were many borderline cases which seemed to be somewhat performative and somewhat informative. Thus he wrote, "the notion of the purity of performative will not survive the transition [to a comprehensive theory of language]."[22] In addition, Austin could never come up with clear-cut criteria of performative utterance, as he sadly notes at the end of his work. Perhaps one of the reasons may be related to the absolute distinction between performative and informative utterances. In my view, in no case *can* there be a performative utterance without informational content. The making of a promise *itself* requires the reporting of what the promise is. Similarly the making of a contract, *itself*, must be a statement of the contract and the ordering of a charge in battle must somehow include information or description of the action created.

In effect, the distinction between performing and informing is probably a fiction, albeit an extremely useful one. What Austin has done is sever the connection between "Doing" (that which is performed) and "Being" (that which is described). But ultimately the two are inseparable and language must somehow reflect that inseparability. However this should not detract from Austin's brilliant insights into the complexity of language and the different levels on which it functions. Most important is the insight that language is capable of doing things in some of its functioning. This insight is of inestimable value for the understanding of law.

It is significant, I believe, that Austin recognized the performative nature of legal language, although his observations on the matter are sparse. He writes that

> it is worth pointing out—reminding you—how many of the 'acts'
> which concern the jurist are or include the utterance of performative,
> or at any rate are or include the performance of some conventional
> procedures.[23]

In holding, this Austin sees legal utterances or pronouncements as essentially performative operating within a set of conventional procedures. Legal pronouncements are not reportive utterances, capable of being true or false as many lawyers have incorrectly stated, he claimed.

A similar view is expressed by John R. Searle in stating his views on the functioning of performative in the broader context of society in general. Searle writes that

> With the exception of supernatural declarations, all declarations bring
> about institutional facts, facts which exist only within systems of
> constitutive rules, and which are, therefore, facts by virtue of human
> agreement.[24]

As does Austin, Searle asserts that social reality is somehow created by declarations or pronouncements in society by a person or body empowered to do so. And as does Austin, he claims that the social facts created are generated within a network of conventional rules and somehow owe their existence to some form of human agreement.

Of the two claims made by Austin and Searle I agree with one and disagree somewhat with the other. It is evident, I agree, that by establishing rules, principles and policies, and by making pronouncements about institutional structures, regulatory agencies, wills, marriage, and trade practices, legislation establishes a social reality. A social world in which individuals are permitted to develop their own private commercial enterprises for their own profit is vastly different from a social world in which only public enterprise and governmental regulation of trade and commerce are permitted. And certainly a society in which the consumption of alcohol is permitted or loosely regulated differs from one in which the consumption of alcohol is a serious criminal offense. By the very legislation enacted, the limits of affluence are affected. In so doing, millionaires and criminals are created. Thus, it would seem social reality is created by legal and other pronouncements functioning as performative utterances.

However I disagree with the view that performative acts occur *only* within a network of conventions and that public agreement is a condition of new social facts. While this may be the case some of the time, it is not the case all of the time. The claims of Austin and Searle are correct in so far as all linguistic utterances are made within a language having agreed upon grammar, syntax, meanings, or whatever else languages need. Without such conventions communication would not be possible. This much is pretty obvious. At another level, a different set of conventions also affects judicial and other social utterances, functioning as performative utterances. For example, the verdict (i.e., a performative utterance) "I find you guilty of travelling at eighty miles per hour in a motor vehicle, in a sixty mph zone" rests on given rules and principles. These rules and principles are among the established conventions in law and their meanings and application are generally agreed upon, if not endorsed. Thus it is possible for individuals as well as the public to agree that certain legal or social conventions exist (e.g., restrictions on smoking) yet oppose their existence.

However, in an equally important way, conventions do not apply to a crucial class of legal and social pronouncements. This is especially so in the case of utterances that serve to break conventions and bring about changes in the status quo. For example, the statement in *The Queen v. Jackson* (1891), "Women are not the chattels of their husbands" not only constituted a break with the recognized conventions of Victorian society, it also *created* a new social reality in which women were no longer chattels. Similarly the statement, "The manufacture, transportation, sale or consumption of all alcoholic beverages is a crime and is prohibited in the U.S. and all its possessions" broke with the existing legal practices in the U.S. and created a new situation in which certain activities, practices, and behaviors were created as criminal activities, practices, and behavior. In neither case did the public endorse the act. And so it is in all new areas such as space law, the realm of electronic communication, fertility practices (e.g., in vitro fertilization, surrogate motherhood), new rules are formulated, new principles enunciated, new practices classified. Some are publicly endorsed, others not. But all (or many) somehow become entrenched in the system.

In effect a new social world is created, a world that in essential respects is a break from the conventions of the earlier world. Thus, not only are there Conventional Performative utterances, that are linguistic statements that do something in their utterance in conformity with the generally agreed upon (though not necessarily endorsed) conventions of that society, in addition, there are Non-Conventional Performative utterances or perhaps Innovative Performative Utterances, which are linguistic utterances, that in their utterance change social reality through the creation of new concepts, rules, principles, policies, and so on. Such statements are context dependent and a statement made at one time may be creative, but the same statement made at another is not. Thus Lord Halsbury stating in 1891 that women are not chattels brought about a fundamental social change. It created a new fact—wives as autonomous persons in the family and not chattels. Such a statement uttered today in Britain would not constitute a change. For the uttering of Innovative Performatives is the primary, if not the only way of effecting social change. Wittgenstein noted, the limits of one's language, including the concepts one uses are the limits of one's reality. Austin went a step further and showed that linguistic statements could do more than describe. Some did things. Some created reality, in their very utterance and under the appropriate conditions both for those who understand and those who do not understand the utterances. All break with past conventions in creating new realities. Some even break with the conventions governing their utterance, as poetry may or as accepting new legal principles such as the validity of certain retroactive legislation may. Law could conceivably declare the basis of its own legitimacy invalid and thereby make all legal conventions invalid.

Through a consideration of the foregoing views of Wittgenstein and Austin, one can begin to understand what happened under Prohibition in the U.S. from 1920 to 1933. How is it that a seemingly rational solution to a serious social problem could bring about such disorder? Why is it that the use of a standard means of social control led to loss of control, that "purifiers became poisoners" and that the work of devout, religious people resulted in corruption? Clearly the beginnings of such explanations must draw from the nature of linguistic acts and their connection to social reality. It has been noted that in functioning performatively, language does something and what it does constitutes a change in the social reality a people or nation lives in. This holds true for all institutional pronouncements of a performative type. This is especially true for law, which is more basic than all institutional forms, except the State, with which it is coextensive. Law thus becomes the basis of other social forms, sets rules for their operation, establishes relationships between individuals and institutions, and, most critically, classifies individuals as criminals and noncriminals. It is through legislation and other rules, through statements of principles or policies justifying verbal and physical actions by the State, and through its judicial verdicts that the State does the foregoing—through its Innovative Performative Utterances.

This is precisely what happened with the enactment of the Volstead Act of 1920. The properly enacted legislation in conformity with the rules and conventions of society transformed society radically. The informal act of having a drink was *transformed* into a criminal act. A social drink for most people was previously a relief from the boredom of work and the anxiety of supporting a family. It was a way of escaping a depressing world, though it created unspeakable misery for some. Yet it was the focus of the only pleasant moments many people had. It was an essential component of a deeply entrenched social ritual as the multitude of saloons and bars prior to Prohibition testify.

However in transforming social reality as it did, the Volstead Act created considerable dislocation and disorientation. It criminalized the livelihood of the manufacturers of alcoholic beverages, salesmen, transporters, workers, and barmen. It interfered with the traditions of many urban immigrant groups. It attempted to disrupt the social lives of many of the young, energetic post-World War I generation. In effect it tried to transform the deeply entrenched reality of many people and instead created a reality more horrifying than the ills that inspired it.

But the emerging reality, I contend was unpredictable. For there was no basis for predicting what would happen. Only in a situation where there is some basis for projecting outcomes from given conditions can this be done. But many or most of the conditions were newly created. Many groups of people in society were redefined or changed and their members *became* something other than they were. What empirical laws and projections could one possible draw on to predict the future? Only with the benefit of hindsight, can we now see that prohibition was bound to fail, and in doing so, it was bound to generate the social disorder felt today.

This fundamental inability to predict and control outcomes of legislation indicates a fundamental indeterminacy in law. Because legal pronouncements are frequently innovative performative in nature, legal rules, verdicts, and other utterances change reality. In this new reality there is no basis for logical induction, thus no basis for prediction. The best one can do is predict on the basis of the categories of the old system. But this will not do because the categories have been transformed, hence are basically different. Thus all one can determine is that he/she cannot really determine outcomes.

But most important, this suggests that some independent noumenal reality exists, something I term Law in Itself. For, something happens—as in the violence, corruption, and disruption of the Prohibition era. What precisely happens cannot be anticipated or predicted in any systematic way. Because we cannot anticipate, we cannot control. Therefore there must be some reality, independent of our knowing as it occurs and independent of our control. This suggests a force over and above our language. Thus there must be a noumenal realm of law. QED, I think.

With the growth of law in recent times, concerns regarding the indeterminacy of law arise. One area of particular concern is that of family law, where considerable legislation has been enacted and radical changes in social relationships brought about. With the ascendancy of a form of humanism within contemporary Western law, discrepancies between women and men in economic, political, marital, and other realms were perceived. In order to rectify long-standing social and personal injustices, Family Reform Acts were designed to give women a fair share of family benefits and to provide women with an equitable and dignified role in marriage. Thus instead of recognizing the husbands' work as the only source of economic well-being of the family, the varieties of women's contributions to the family economy were recognized. Ultimately changes of this sort led to a basic redefinition of marriage as a union of economic equals.[25]

As a moral position, such documents are laudable. They constitute rational responses to moral and social problems. They directly attack grave social injustices and point in newer, fairer directions. However when one probes beneath the surface and considers what is really done by such acts, the rationality and good intentions of the acts may seem secondary in importance. As statements with performative force, such laws modify and recreate social reality. Specifically they redefine, hence change a fundamental human relationship. A highly personal spontaneous and unjust (unfair) relationship of unequals has been replaced by a more just (fair) economic, legal relationship of equals. Though it is still too early to tell, there is considerable evidence to support the possibility that such laws will contribute to the abolition of the family as it exists today. To make the family economic, formal and highly contractual is not simply to modify it; it is to create a new social form.

A possible irony in all this is that in its very statement and by its very existence, such an act may render its aim unrealizable. Though its aim may be to rectify inequalities in the family, there may not be a family in the same sense, in which women can become equals. This may or may not be a good thing, but because the outcome is unknowable, it is a risky thing—as all innovative legislation is. But the point is that law may have brought about changes, unwittingly, and by virtue of its own ineffable existence, that went far beyond its intentions, and created conditions that made its aims unattainable. In other words, the proclaimed objectives of this sort of legislation may be unattainable in the reality created by the legislation. Just as legislated sobriety led to orgies of drinking and corruption, so legislated economic families may lead to a different form of family or no family at all. Yet in its wisdom, by fiat, the Ontario legislature—as have many others in the Western world—has created a new social unit, the economic, legal, contractual family. At this time, where "the family" is going, what it will develop, is not determinable. No basis for projection exists. But something quite independent of our thinking, planning, and execution is going on.

A number of similar points have been made by Ellen Wilson in an article addressing itself to broader feminist issues. On Wilson's view, the law is severely restricted in what it can do in promoting the welfare of women and safeguarding their rights. Because of the unintended consequences that are likely to follow the enactment of some of the legislation to promote such rights, law is the wrong instrument for the operation. She notes that

> One great political truth which should be engraved on every legislator's heart is this: every law does more than it is supposed to do. Every law spills over into areas it was never intended to affect. Like St. Paul, every legislator can confess that he has done that which he would not do.[26]

That she has pointed to a "great truth" is amply supported by the events of Prohibition. Wilson would undoubtedly add that laws promoting women's welfare and rights also provide support.

Wilson's explanation of the unintended, negative effects of law is that legislators tend to focus on the group it targets and often ignore other groups associated with the target group. For example,

> when courts handle divorce settlements as they would the dissolution of a business partnership, they dilute the distinctive function of marriage as an institution entrusted with the bearing and nurturing of children.[27]

In such cases the effect of treating marriage as a union of economic equals is to destroy the basic procreative and nurturing function of the family and this will have considerable effect on the children, often devastating effect. Thus Wilson criticizes much in feminist legal programs because they suffer from tunnel vision and ignore the rights and welfare of other groups in society. She also criticizes the purely technical and economic approach to handling divorce settlements. This approach is fundamentally inadequate.

> What is missing is a social change of heart—an internal assent of the mind and heart accompanying the externally enforced change of public behaviour.[28]

Wilson is undoubtedly justified in insisting that legislatures not cave in to the pressures of any interest group without considering the effects on the welfare and rights of all associated groups affected by their demands. She is also reasonable in pointing out that purely formal adherence to law is not enough and that a change of heart is also needed. The problem that I find with these eminently sensible suggestions is that they are unrealizable. One cannot know beforehand who will be affected by a radically new type of legislation, nor can one know how or when they will be affected. All we can really know is that a very profound change in society has occurred, a change in the nature of groups and actions. Moreover, insisting that legislation in a complex, multicultural, post-industrial society be accompanied by a change of heart by its members is asking more of legislators, let alone ordinary human beings, that one ought to. Changes of heart, I believe are beyond both coronary surgery and the law. It is even beyond the manipulation of psychiatrist and psychologists, though some would deny it.

An area in which law and the human heart frequently come into conflict is in the area of human rights. It is possible that the new Charter of Rights, entrenched in the New Canadian Constitution will have a similar effect of helping to create a new social reality. In legislating tolerance, and by threatening sanctions against the intolerant, the Charter of Rights may make basic social relationships, formal and legal. Previously, tolerance was considered to be a human attitude that reflected the respect of one person for another, the recognition of one's natural rights as a human being to make certain choices, and so on. Now tolerance is defined for us in terms of what may or may not be said and may or may not be done. It requires no personal affirmation of another person's humanity. It only requires conformity to regulations. Legislated tolerance constitutes a radical change in that it affects how we view others and relate to them. This may be for the good, to the extent that it controls some of the nasty verbal and physical abuse of bigots. But it has transformed our worlds in more ways and on more levels than legislators have conceived. It affects those it does not intend to affect, as Ellen Wilson noted. And it is basically indeterminate in its outcomes, meanings, and implications, as there is no knowing its consequences. In effect, it could create a society in which basically intuitive and spontaneous modes of relating to others are replaced by conformity to predefined behavioral rules in a law-soaked society.

Concluding Remarks

In conclusion, it would seem that law is a distinctive type of institution, whose workings are understandable at some levels, but inaccessible at others. Law has an inner dynamic of its own that is independent of the intentions of the framers of laws. This inner dynamic is complex and its workings largely indeterminable. But some general, nonsubstantive features of Law in Itself may be discernible. In addition to having the Parkinsonian trait of growing and growing until it is rendered immobile and of developing mechanisms of control and self-perpetuation, as other institutions do, law has the feature of creating new social relationships and other social realities through its enactments. Because of the performative nature of the language of law, such new realities can be created. Ironically, once the legislators have performed their act of creation, they are deprived of much of their power. In the context of the new reality, there is no basis for predicting the outcome of the legislation, and without such knowledge, control is not possible. Thus a new reality is created, but how it functions and where it goes is beyond its creators. In effect, it seems to have a life of its own, an inner dynamic of its own, quite apart from the intentions of legislators.

Legislation is always a risky business. The rules thereby enacted always affect reality. New rules change reality. Radically new rules change reality radically. Because of the crucial role that rules play in social existence, the analogy between life (or law) and games is somewhat apt. But it is only an analogy, not a full description of either games or life (or law). For rules in life and law change as life and law unfold; but rules of games remain static as the games unfold. In both life and games, the rules are made up or "constructed", as sociologists tell us. Rules are ours. However, the form they take, how they unfold or what they do is not ours. Human control in life and law, especially, is limited, because life and law are indeterminate. Prediction is not possible. And therein lies the risk.

Thus I have contended that such legislation as a prohibition act, a family reform act or a charter of rights may, in some contexts, radically alter social reality. Not only are wives made equal economic partners, members of minority groups given the right to practice their cultures and religions or the drinking of alcoholic beverages prohibited; but the very *ways* these matters are conceived are altered. These matters are moved from the realm of the private, the personal, and the spontaneous to the realm of the public, controlled, scrutinized legal order. These matters and the attendant relationships are no longer the same. What happens in each of these realms is novel, hence basically different.

The growing tendency in our society to deal with problems in a formal, legal way is an offshoot of the great rational myth of our age that we can control nature for our declared purposes. Law, clearly, is one of the major instruments of social control today. We seem to be caught up in the process of using this powerful means whether or not there are grounds for believing it will work. But not only does it frequently not work, it is itself a factor in creating a situation where working is impossible. Because of the nature of its language, there is indeterminacy, and if somehow desirable results follow legal enactments, the results themselves cannot be attributed to the enactments. Of course, you cannot tell this to politicians who will always take credit for positive results and explain away social failures "rationally."

As a consequence of recent family and other social legislation, many of the choices that individuals have made in the context of family, in social transactions, in economic dealings are no longer available. Though changes in the family may have been enacted democratically, they were enacted without a realization of the deeper meaning and significance of the change. It may be argued by legal apologists that the choices no longer available (e.g., economic dominance by one spouse) are no losses to society. But this is not the point. How people relate to one another, socially, sexually and so on is changed beyond recall. Our worlds, our ways of conceiving the world have also been changed beyond recall. We have been robbed of spontaneity and intuition in our dealings with others, and not simply prevented from doing bad things to one another.

It is quite possible, then, that the use of law to change social reality is a major violation of human rights, greater in scope, perhaps, than anything else. For it has taken away from all the right to make choices as we wish, by *imposing* on us a new world, and more significantly, a new mode of dealing with the world. The imposition of such restrictions may not be deliberate, but the restrictions are inherent in the legalistic mode of imposing them, whether we recognize this or not.

But is there any alternative? Surely, after generations of abuse, women should be guaranteed a fair share of joint property and be protected from the indignities due to an unequal status? Surely not to act is a form of action, an ineffectual or dangerous one at that? Obviously this line of argumentation has considerable force. When confronted with intolerable problems that never seem to go away, one does not refuse to act because the acting may create conditions that are unknowable. This would certainly be the case where the very existence of a group or of society is threatened.

However, it is important to disabuse ourselves of certain illusions and to have a better idea of the limits and dangers of the inner workings of law. Law is not an unmixed blessing. In some instances, it has been used to solve social problems or remove a threat to society. In the past, laws have served to protect children from unscrupulous factory owners, to protect tenants from landlords, to prevent the consumption of alcohol from devastating society (in eighteenth-century England) and on and on. In other instances, it created more problems than it solved. What is important to realize is that one should not view law as a reliable method of social improvement, let alone a fail-safe method. The consequences of law cannot be known beforehand, because specific laws and the overall use of law change reality. Law itself is growing as a means of dealing with problems and this itself affects our manner of thinking and the very way we deal with reality. If this does stifle spontaneity and intuition, as I suggested, and if a loss of spontaneity and intuitive response coupled with an increase in ordered, rational thinking is an indication of social and cultural decline, as Spengler speculated, then law may ultimately serve to accentuate the process of decline and corruption that it is supposed to counter.

Thus we may be faced with an irresolvable dilemma. If we don't use law to solve social problems and rectify injustices, the problems and injustices will likely continue or even get worse. If, on the other hand, we do use law as the dominant means of solving our social problems, we accentuate the sterile rationalism that is paralyzing our society. In the first case, we become swamped by conditions we refuse to control and in the second we create situations over which we have no control. Obviously we must do one or the other. In my view the risky second option is usually better than the first, though perhaps not always. In any case, one should try to know what one can about law—if only to know better whether and when to duck. One should recognize that law is more than a system of rules and more than the historical unfolding of phenomena and patterns. Law is a fundamental social institution, encompassing all others, that defines social reality and unfolds according to its own inner dynamic. The definition may be done by "us," but the unfolding is done by "it." The more radically we redefine our reality, the more we believe we are in control, but are in fact the more disoriented. For that reason revolutionary programs are usually the riskiest. In their near total redefinition of social forms and social relationships, revolutionaries lose their ground for anticipating even specific events in the future. And in their attempt to perpetuate their own existence, as do all institutions, especially governments, they rely on the oppressive methods of their predecessors. If this is so, revolutions are justified only in the most extreme situation of hopelessness. Almost never.

How, then, are we to understand the workings of law at all its levels? Unfortunately our educational system has no way of dealing with a phenomenon as complex and elusive as law. Education is too often confined to linear modes of understanding, to the rational and classifiable. It rarely undertakes to view itself critically or probe into its own assumptions. Occasionally it deals with a long-range process of development. It never deals with the nonrational or the indeterminate. It never deals with the larger process that spawns rationality (or, of course, irrationality). It never deals with the dealing, the process of doing as doing not as done, analyzed, and classified. I call this unfortunate, because the nonrational and indeterminable are not only part of human existence, they function at a level prior to rationality and determinacy. The rational and determinate did not arise out of nowhere.

The final question in this section now becomes, "How does one deal with the nonrational, the indeterminable, the virtually inaccessible?" To answer this, I have no formula. For there is no formula for dealing with that which is prior to the formal. In any event, any answer to this question can at this stage only be very general and only suggest the limits of understanding.

That which we try to grasp—or at least to make some cognitive contact with-is the thing itself. Merely dealing with the constructs we devise leaves too much unanswered. It fails to deal with the constant breakdowns of our rational systems, especially the law. If there is a Thing In Itself or Law Itself or Nature Itself it cannot be, as Kant insisted, beyond the realm of possible experience. It cannot be totally beyond the categories of being and causing. It must exist and it must affect. Thus whatever the noumenon is, it must make contact with human experience and somehow be known to do so.

So it is with Law In Itself. We believe it exists and it affects us because rational solutions are carried down irrational whirlpools in ways beyond our possible knowing. There must be something beyond our experience and beyond the concepts we contrive. From my musings and speculations, this noumenal reality is manifested in various partially contrived social structures. They are found in the institutional, where institutions have lives of their own. They are found in the human mind, where the mind as grasper emerges, prior to classification and packaging. They are manifested in the social structures created by language functioning performatively. They are found in the methods we use, causing them to break down when they do not mesh with reality. But more will be said about these in the final chapter.

The upshot of all this, is that in education we should strive to gain an understanding not only of the here and now with generally accepted devices, but to gain an understanding of the devices being used. Thus social reality or nature should not simply be viewed as a social construct, a fiction humans invent. It should involve understanding the nature and limits of those devices. Thus social reality must take into account the institutions under which that reality is studied and the internal dynamics of that institution. It must take into account the rational method it employs and the limits of that method. It must also consider the functioning of the mind as active agent in the process. And finally it must take into account the language used to create social reality, the manner in which it functions and its limits.

Overall this does not come out to be very much. We may know very generally that there are social constructs and a reality in itself. For more than constructs are involved. However we know precious little about reality. In law, we know that ultimately there is an indeterminacy in this law, because human constructs can never take themselves into consideration. When they try to, they transform the active striving in itself into a passive structure observed. There are limits to human knowledge and it is important to know what they are, if we are to avoid trying to know what cannot be known and trying to do what cannot be done. This should be the first lesson drilled into law students, lawyers, judges and legislators. Then we should hope and pray that they learn.

Notes

1. I. Kant, *The Critique of Pure Reason*, 7.
2. M. McLuhan, *Understanding Media*.
3. M. McLuhan, "Education in the Electronic Age," *Interchange*, 1, 2, (1970), 2.
4. Oswald Spengler, *The Decline of the West* (New York: Modern Library, 1962), 7ff.
5. L. Wittgenstein, *Tractatus Logico-Philosophicus* (36:5.4711).
6. Ibid., 5.62.
7. L. Wittgenstein, *Philosophical Investigations* (37, II, 11).
8. P. Winch, *The Idea of a Social Science*, 15.
9. L. Wittgenstein, *Tractatus Logico-Philosophicus*, 7, 151.
10. In recent years a multitude of articles have appeared in Canada and the U.S. warning about the consequences of such overload. These include articles by the Canadian minister of justice, the chief justice of the Supreme Court of the U.S.A. and other prominent officials.
11. See E. Goffman, *Asylums* and I. Illich, *Deschooling Society*.
12. Quoted in *The Toronto Globe and Mail*, 13 Apr. 1982, 17.
13. *The Volstead Act* (1920).
14. Andrew Sinclair, *Prohibition: The Era of Excess*, 37 ff.
15. B. Sunday, *Billy Sunday Speaks*.
16. Ibid., 54.
17. *Ibid.*, 56.
18. Sinclair, *Prohibition*, viii.
19. Peter C. Newmann, *The Bronfman Dynasty: The Rothschilds of the New World*, 83.
20. *Ibid.*, 22.
21. See *Philosophical Papers*, ed. J. Urmson, "Other Minds" *P.A.S.* Supp. vol. XX (1946) and *How to Do Things With Words*.
22. *How To Do Things With Words*, 150.
23. Ibid., p. 19.
24. John R. Searle, *Intentionality: An Essay on the Philosophy of Mind*, 172.
25. *Ontario Family Reform Act*, 1978, R.S.O. 1978.
26. Ellen Wilson, *"Women and the Law," Update on law related education*. New York, Fall 1981, 19.
27. Ibid.
28. Ibid., 21.

7

Summary and Final Comments

Now that my musings are done—at least for now—what do they all come down to? What sense can I make of what I have written? On first reflection, I seem to say many different things about many different subjects. But do they share a common thread, a basic conception?

If pressed, I might come up with a general thesis about knowledge and control. This thesis would state that there is a fundamental indeterminacy to social knowledge. That is, there are some critical determining aspects of society and social relationships that are beyond human knowing, that are inaccessible to the instruments of knowledge that we are obliged to have and use. Because it is impossible to know such things as the nature of reality, the nature of the instruments we possess, and the impact of our own reflections and involvements, we can never control any significant outcomes of our actions. So in spite of the assurances of the snake oil salesmen of our day—among them some politicians, futurologists,[1] and con men with schemes for becoming rich, powerful, and totally in control of our psychic and physical behavior—it is impossible to control our destinies. For we are inadequately equipped to do so, and some outside (and inside) realities do not permit us to do so.

It would seem that in examining and reflecting on social behavior, on human relationships and endeavors, on human thought, on social institutions and social conditions, that there are several kinds of indeterminacy. Because there is some apparent overlap of these elements, it is difficult to establish whether there are five or more types of indeterminacy. But in any case, each would go some way in explaining why "the best laid plans of mice and men gang aft agley"—why there is so great a discrepancy between what we plan and where we end up. Rationalists will obsessively look for technical flaws in our procedures. But in doing so they totally ignore their own functioning and the functioning of the context of social behavior in social existence.

169

At the outset of this work, I focused on the role of mind in indeterminacy. It may well be that because of the absolutely basic role of mind in all knowledge, that the nature of mind is somehow at the root of indeterminacy. Whether this is so or not, one thing becomes evident. Mind, consciousness, awareness, "seeing," grasping can only apprehend something other than itself knowing, being aware, being conscious, and so on. Kant recognized this problem and tried to skirt it by assuming that the self recognizes itself from an examination of its own accomplishments. However in so doing, Kant ignores the self (i.e., an aware mind) recognizing its own accomplishments. He referred to the products of a self and observed the self that produced the products, but he did not account for his own observing and producing—nor could he. Inferring a self from its products (whatever that means) is not knowing a self knowing. Such inferences are one level removed from the dynamic act of knowing. As I noted repeatedly an eye cannot see an eye seeing; a hand cannot grasp itself grasping. Similarly, a mind cannot know a mind knowing. Yet such knowing is part of reality. That much we know! And because of this there must be a fundamental social indeterminacy. There are some aspects of society, some level of conscious human beings functioning that are inaccessible to human knowledge. Thus the view that we can control social development is false, a myth.

A second form of indeterminacy is the indeterminacy in science, which is most readily acknowledged at the level of subatomic reactions or phenomena. On this principle ("the uncertainty principle"), it is not possible to determine the motion and position of a subatomic particle at one time. The explanation for this that is commonly provided to the public is that the instruments of measurement themselves intrude upon the measurement of microscopic events. Just as the insertion of a very large, very cold thermometer into a test tube of a warm liquid will affect the temperature reading of that liquid, so the use of any measuring device will affect not only readings of motion and position but also the possibility of measuring both motion and position simultaneously. In effect, one must use measuring devices in order to determine the physical qualities of nature. But the use of such devices themselves affect one's findings, as well as limit the qualities that can be determined. For this reason, the instruments of measurement are seen not as neutral devices for understanding nature but actually as constituting physical nature, as Heisenberg has claimed.[2] Thus for physicists there is no independently existing nature, waiting out there to be discovered. The technology humans use, that is the extensions of their eyes and other senses, finds its way into nature and is reflected in the concepts of nature we have as well as in the specific descriptions physicists present. It also finds its way into the social reality we live in. As a result, a complex phenomenon of indeterminacy arises. On the one hand, mind is a constituent feature of social reality that is indeterminable. On the other hand, mind is a necessary guiding force in the development of all technologies of natural and social science, some of which, at least, are factors in physical indeterminacy. It would seem that no matter what level of knowledge we are involved in, some sort of indeterminacy results.

A third source of indeterminacy, intricately related to the first, and second, pertains to the rational mode of dealing with others, problems, the world. In choosing and using rationality we buy into a system of methods and beliefs. The central belief is that there are proper rational modes of procedure that include reasoning according to specific logical paradigms, paradigms outlined by the likes of Aristotle, Russell, Quine, von Wright, and others. These paradigms may represent correct deductive, inductive, modal, and practical types of reasoning. In effect, there are knowable connections between premises about actions taken in this world and conclusions about desirable outcomes. If so, planning correct procedures to achieve goals is possible on this view. Thus rational people analyze problems into constituent parts, decide on plausible goals in the context, reflect on prevailing conditions and known general laws covering those conditions, then decide on the most effective, acceptable means of achieving the desired goals. Reliance on prejudice, superstition, whim, blind chance is minimized. Rather, one proceeds with one's eyes open, constantly reflecting on the proven mode of rational procedure. It is only by going this way that we can control the events of social lives as well as large social phenomena.

One of the most influential proponents of rationalism was the American philosopher, John Dewey. For Dewey, the scientific method of constantly testing and retesting hypotheses, for achieving desired goals is the only rational method for dealing with problems and this method "is the only authentic means at our command for getting at the significance of our everyday experience of the world in which we live."[3] The psychologist B. F. Skinner has even claimed that the great progress in medicine and science over the past four hundred years was tied to the use of a rational scientific methodology.[4]

However I do not believe that rationality is an unmixed blessing. Perhaps in many situations, if not most, the use of rational methods leads to more effective and satisfying outcomes than being driven by alternative irrational modes. But there are frequently severe limitations on rational method. In the preceding chapters I outlined two distinct sorts of limitation in rational method that reduce or nullify its utility. In chapter 3, I noted that using General Problem Solving Models fails at least half the time when two rational individuals or groups are locked into a conflict in which each is trying to outmaneuver or vanquish the other. Up to a ceratin point, rationality may be useful. For example, in a war situation one aligns troops, in certain ways, protects one's flanks, utilizes topography in the deployment of troops and employs generally effective tactics and strategies. However, ultimately, at a crucial juncture, two minds are in battle, each trying to fathom the reasoning of the other and the response of the other, to his fathoming of the other, *ad infinitum*. The process has no end, the factors are indeterminate. As a result rationality plays no role at this level of interaction. Possibly, intuition does. That is having a gut feeling of what your opponents will do, how they will react or respond. But there can be no statistics to back the gut feeling.

A second sort of limitation on rationality was discussed in chapter 6. There I took the position that rationality is not simply an active mode of determining one's destiny. Rationality may be a determinant in some instances. But it may also be an ingredient in social reality, itself determined by other forces. Rationality may be, as Spengler claimed, a feature of declining civilizations and an indication of the inability of a civilization to stem the erosion of its strength and vitality. Certainly there is ample evidence in our legal system, where new laws and principles are incessantly produced to categorize and control social behavior, that rationality may lead to a breakdown of the system, with the disruption of social relationships and the burnout of the judiciary. Thus there may be a larger process in which rationality is merely a small passive part. Our believing that we control our destiny by rational planning is much like the behaviorist's mouse believing it has created a supply system of food pellets by running the maze (or pressing the right lever). If we and our rationality are the mice of the system, then there is a significant indeterminacy in the social world we inhabit, at least from the human perspective.

A fourth type of indeterminacy may be due to the nature of social institutions and the way they operate. Goffman has pointed out that in total institutions there is a discrepancy between what the administrators say they are doing and what actually happens. Regardless of the clear statements of ideals and the setting up of effective mechanisms for achieving these ideals, total institutions develop lives of their own where control takes precedence over therapy, education, or growth and where clear distinctions between staff and clients or inmates occur. All the rational analysis and planning of administration is of no avail in a situation where the warehousing and manipulation of clients is an immediate necessity. Similarly, Ivan Illich denounced schooling, because the hierarchical structure carried with it a materialistic, undemocratic, antihumanistic ethic. It makes no difference whether the school is run by rational humanists or irrational fascists, the result is always the same. My personal experience in working on a training school program is consistent with these views, though I believe that the situation goes beyond simple control and a monolithic system. For institutions do vary in types of control and even conviviality. But in any case, rational planning and careful analysis or study cannot ultimately grasp the workings of institutions (total or partial) nor can they guarantee predetermined outcomes.

Finally, a fifth type of indeterminacy can be attributed to the nature and function of language, especially legal language. In chapter 6, I claimed that attempts to understand law as a system of rules and to understand it as an historical process are not adequate. Both miss an aspect of law that is crucial. In addition, I claimed that there is something I call "Law in itself" or "Noumenal Law" that is suggested by the fact that conscious, controlled, well-conceived, "rational" attempts to generate laws to control social behavior often lead to disastrous social consequences as the Prohibition Act did, as drug laws seem to be doing and as family reform acts and anti-hate legislation may do. Such legislation radically transforms social reality. It creates a strange new world in which social activities, basic values and common practices are redefined. Because much legal language functions performatively, because its very utterance creates new forms, values, and realities, the members of society become disoriented. They have no basis for predicting the outcomes of their actions. There is, also, no basis for projecting the outcomes of such changes because they are radically new. In effect, because new rules are introduced, and rules are performative utterances, and there are no grounds for comprehending the meaning and operation of the rules, a pervasive social indeterminacy results. Rational planning and behavior make no difference. They did not make a difference during Prohibition. Nor can we know when it will ever make a difference.

If indeed, there are five sorts of indeterminacy in social knowledge and each is somehow distinctive and derives from a different source, a couple of questions remain. First, are there only five sorts? Is there any reason to believe that the list is exhaustive and that other sorts are impossible or unlikely? The more important question, however is, what is the connection amongst the five forms of indeterminacy that I suggested?

To the first, I can only respond that I do not know. Though there appears to be some relationship between the indeterminacies of mind, rationality, and language, there are also differences in each. They do not all operate at the same level of understanding. Mind is the most basic; rationality seems to be a function of mind; and language can be seen both as a function and constituent. I cannot really argue the matter at this time, but there do not seem to be grounds for reducing the number. On the other hand, I cannot see that the five sorts are exhaustive of indeterminacies. In effect, it may not be possible to determine the extent of indeterminacy in social understanding. Which seems to make sense.

With regard to the connection between the five sorts of indeterminacy, I cannot give a specific answer. The subject could possibly be a fruitful focus of future inquiry. However, it is possible to give a general answer to the question. It would be as follows.

In all five cases the means or instruments needed to acquire knowledge or to do something (i.e., achieve a goal) consciously or deliberately obtrude upon the process, in the sense of becoming a part of the process, while at the same time remaining distinct. Mind is a necessary condition for any knowledge, any system of knowledge, and all conscious behavior, yet it acts in a way that makes it part of every social process. In science, the instruments of measurement are said by Heisenberg to constitute the very nature studied. Rationality, as well, is a means or mode or method of knowing, yet it is an ingredient in the social reality studied. Institutions are the means or instruments for providing services that bring about social ideals and goals. They are also part of the process in which the goals are supposed to be realized. And finally language is the means of creating the reality that must be understood to control social outcomes. It is also part of that reality. It constitutes the reality. Of course the means involved in the various areas are different. Minds and thermometers are very different, as are rational structures and institutions. And language is different for all the others, yet intricately connected.

In a limited but suggestive way, the McLuhan chestnut, "The Medium is the Message" captures the idea. Even though it is an overstatement, since messages go beyond the instrument conveying them, it does bring out the idea that the means of expressing or doing constitutes what is known. How one says or does anything determines, in some sense, what is said or done. Messages require media to exist,[5] and media require messages to exist. But when the medium itself serves as conveyor but at the same time is conveyed and is part of the subject studied, indeterminacy results. It (i.e., the medium) cannot be used to know itself knowing. It cannot serve a double purpose, one of which requires stepping out of its own feet. So there is a reality or level of reality out there beyond our grasping and it is either suggested by or the result of the means we use to achieve ends.

One final question—with four sub-questions. What can we know?

1.   Can we know everything about everything? To this we can answer with complete assurance, "No!" Given the fact that uncertainty and indeterminacy and incompletability prevail in science then complete knowledge is an impossibility. It would appear that not even God can know everything about everything, nor as a result do everything and anything. So much for omniscience and omnipotence.

2.   Can we know something about everything? This is a more difficult question because it may be possible to state conditions or limits for all Being—even if it is knowledge about the indeterminacy pervading all knowledge. However we do not know whether we can be aware of all forms of existence or whether indeterminacy applies to all. The possibility is infinitesimal, if that.

3.   Can we know everything about something? No! To know anything requires an instrument or means of knowing. In which case indeterminacy must enter. If so, we cannot grasp our grasping, which somehow must affect the object studied.

4.   Finally, can we know something about something? Clearly, yes! Read this book! Then you would know something.

Something about the present; perhaps less about the past; but little about the future that can count as knowledge and not as a lucky guess. In all cases, we can at least know that we cannot know. But this was said by Socrates over 2400 years ago.

Notes

1. See M. Dublin, *Futurehype*, Penguin Books, Toronto, 1989 for an account of the dreadful track record of futurologists.
2. Von Heisenberg, *The Physicist's Conception of Nature*, 5.
3. Dewey, *Experience and Education*, p. 188.
4. Skinner, *Beyond Freedoom and Dignity*, chap. 1, 1-23.
5. With the possible exception of Intuitive Knowledge. However even this is unclear because intuitive knowledge may require a language, not only for its expression, but possibly for its existence.

Bibliography

Austin, J. 1962, 1975. *How To Do Things With Words*, J.O.Urmson and M. Sbisa, eds. Oxford University Press, Oxford, New York.

Blackstone, W. 1973. *Commentaries on the Laws of England.* In The Sovereignty *of The Law*, G. Jones, ed. Toronto: University of Toronto Press.

Bourne, P. T. and J. A. Eisenberg, 1978. *Social Issues in the Curriculum.* Toronto: OISE Press.

Bredemeier, B. J. and D. L. Shields, 1985. "Values and Violence in Sports Today." *Psychology Today*, October 1985.

Brown, I 1984. "Thinking Without a Brain." *The Globe and Mail*, Toronto, 6 October 1984.

Bruner, J. S. 1966. *The Process of Education.* Cambridge, Mass.: Harvard University Press.

The Charter of Rights and Freedoms: A Guide for Canadians. 1984. Ottawa: Publications Canada.

Collingwood, R.G. 1962. *The Idea of History.* New York, Oxford: Galaxy Books, Oxford University Press.

Dennett, D.C. 1984. "Computer Models and the Mind: A View from the East Pole." *Psychology and Artificial Intelligence.* 14 December 1984.

Dewey, J. 1933. *How We Think: A Restatement of the Relation of Reflective Thinking to the Educative Process.* Boston: D.C. Heath.

Dewey J. 1963. *Experience and Education.* New York: Collier.

Dublin, M. 1989. *Futurehype: The Tyranny of Prophecy.* Markham, Ontario: Viking.

Dworkin, R. 1977. *Taking Rights Seriously.* Cambridge, Mass.: Harvard University Press.

Eisenberg, J. A. and M.A. Levin., eds. 1972-80 eds. Toronto: Canadian
    Critical Issues Series, General Publishers, Don Mills, Ontario and OISE
    Press.

Eisenberg, J. A. 1984. "Canadian Public Issues Program." *Ethics and
    Education,* Toronto: OISE Press, 3, 8 (April 1984).

Eisenberg, J. A. 1987. "In Defence of the Canadian Public Issues Approach to
    Values Education." *Interchange.* 18, 4, (April 1984) Toronto: OISE
    Press.

Fuller, L.L. 1975. *The Morality of Law.* New Haven, Conn.: Yale University
    Press.

Gervais, C.H. 1984. The *Rumrunners.* Scarborough, Ontario: Firefly Books.
    Scarborough, Ontario.

Goffman, E. 1961. *Asylums: Essays on the Social Situations of Mental Patients
    and Other Inmates.* Hammondsworth: Penguin Books.

Hart, H. L. A. 1961. *The Concept of Law.* London, New York: Oxford
    University Press.

Heisenberg, W.   1958. *The Physicist's Conception of Nature.*   London:
    Hutchinson, University Library.

Heisenberg, W.   1962, *Physics that Philosophy: The Revolution in Modern
    Science.* New York: Harper and Row.

Hornbeck, P. 1980, "Doing Justice to Legal Education." *Quill and Quire* 46,
    5 (May 1980).

Illich, I.   1971,   "The Alternative to Schooling." *Saturday Review,* 19 June
    1971.

Illich, I. 1972. *Deschooling Society.* New York: Harper and Row.

Jackendoff, R. 1987. *Consciousness and the Computational Mind.* Cambridge:
    MIT Press.

Johnson-Laird, P.A.   1988. *The Computer and the Computational Mind: An
    Introduction to Cognitive Science,* Cambridge, Mass.:   Harvard
    University Press.

Kant, I. 1956. *The Critique of Pure Reason.* Trans. N. K. Smith, London:
    MacMillan Co.

Kant, I. 1956. *The Moral Law*. Trans. H. J. Paton, third edition, London: Hutchinson University Library.

Kirschenbaum, H. 1977. Cambrigde: "In Support of Values Clarification." *Social Education*, May 1977.

Kohlberg, L., P. Scharf, and J. Hickey, 1977. "The Justice Structure of the Prison: A Theory and Intervention." *The Prison Journal* 51, 2 (1972)

Kohlberg, L. 1981. *The Philosophy of Moral Development*, New York: Harper and Row.

Krug, M. 1967. *History and Social Science*. Waltham, Mass.: Blaisdell Publications.

Kuhn, T.S. 1966. *The Structure of Scientific Revolutions*. Chicago: Phoenix Books.

Levi, E. H. 1948. *An Introduction to Legal Reasoning*. Chicago: University of Chicago Press.

McLuhan, H. M. 1964. *Understanding Media: The Extensions of Man*, second edition, New York: Signet Books.

McLuhan, H. M. 1968. *The Gutenberg Galaxy*. Toronto: University of Toronto Press.

Minsky, M. 1985. *The Society of Mind*. New York: Simon and Schuster.

Nagel, E. and J. R. Newman. 1956 "Goedels' Proof." In *The World of Mathematics*, Vol. 3 J. R. Newman, ed. New York: Simon and Schuster.

Newell, A. and H. A. Simon 1963. "G. P. S., A Program That Simulates Human Thought." In *Computers and Thought*, E.A. Feigenbaum and J. Felman eds. New York: McGraw Hill.

Newmann, F. 1970. *Clarifying Public Controversy: An Approach to Teaching Social Studies*. Boston: Little Brown Co.

Newmann, P.C. 1978. *Bronfman Dynasty: the Rothschilds of the New World*. Toronto: McLelland and Stewart.

Oliver, D. and J. Shaver. 1966. *Teaching Public Issues in the High School*. Boston: Houghton, Mifflin Co.

Penrose, R. 1989. *The Emperor's New Mind*. Oxford, New York: Oxford University Press.

Pylyshyn, Z. 1984. *Computation and Cognition.* Cambridge: MIT Press.

Raths, L.E., M. Harman, and S. B. Simon. 1960, *Values and Teaching*, first edition. New York: Charles Merrill.

Rudner, R. 1966. *The Philosophy of the Social Sciences.* Englewood Cliffs, N.J.: Prentice Hall, Inc.

Searle, J. R. 1983. *Intentionality: An Essay in the Philosophy of Mind.* Cambridge: Cambridge University Press.

Simon, S.B., L. W. Howe and H. Kirschenbaum 1978. *Values Clarification: A Handbook of Practical Strategies for Teachers and Students.* Revised Edition. New York: Hart Publishing.

Sinclair, A. 1962. *Prohibition: The Era of Excess.* Boston: Little, Brown.

Skinner, B. F. 1972. *Beyond Freedom and Dignity.* New York: Bantam, Vintage Books.

Spengler, O. 1962. *The Decline of the West.* Trans. C.F. Atkinson, abridged edition. New York: The Modern Library.

Sunday, W. 1981. *Billy Sunday Speaks.* K. Gullin, ed. New York: Chelsea House Publishers.

Wilson, E. 1981. "Women and the Law." *Update on Law Related Education.* Fall, 1981.

Winch, P. 1967. *The Idea of a Social Science.* London: Routledge and Kegan Paul.

Wittgenstein, L. 1961. *Tractatus Logico-Philosophicus.* Trans. D. F. Pears and B. F. McGuinness. London: New York: Routledge and Kegan Paul.

Wittgenstein, L. 1968. *Philosophical Investigations.* Trans. G.E.M. Anscombe. Oxford: Basil Blackwell.

Young, G.M. 1964. *Victorian England: Portrait of an Age.* London: Oxford University Press.

Index